WE STILL CALL HIM COACH

WE STILL CALL HIM COACH

THE LIFE AND LEGACY OF LES HABEGGER

DORIS H. PIEROTH

CROSS TRAINING PUBLISHING

Cross Training Publishing
PO Box 1874
Kearney, Nebraska 68848

Individual sales: This book is available through most bookstores or can be ordered directly from Cross Training Publishing at the address above.

Quantity Sales: Special discounts are available on quantity purchases by corporations, associations and others. For details, contact the "Special Sales Department" at the publisher's address above.

Edited by Dave Lindstedt
Cover Design by Lori Shimizu
Interior Design by Kira Fulks • www.kirafulks.com

Library of Congress Cataloging-in-Publication Data is available from the publisher

ISBN: 978-1-929478-67-5

Printed in the United States of America

CONTENTS

About the Author

Doris H. Pieroth of Seattle holds a PhD in history from the University of Washington. She is the author of numerous journal articles and five books, including the acclaimed *Their Day in the Sun: Women of the 1932 Olympics* (Seattle: University of Washington Press, 1996). In 2008 she received the Washington State Historical Society's highest award for lifetime achievement. As a historian and sports fan, Dr. Pieroth welcomed the opportunity to tell Les Habegger's multifaceted and inspiring story.

Author's Note

Though not a conventional biography, this is the life story of Les Habegger, one of basketball's more successful yet unsung coaches. It is a memoir, but written from a third-person perspective, as befits a man who has remained modest throughout his life, even as he accomplished more than most men in sports ever dream of. This account is based on more than thirty hours of interviews I had with Coach Habegger, and on papers from his personal files; it is his view of events as his life unfolded.

In order to provide background and context for this remarkable story, I have tapped other sources as well, including members of the Habegger family, friends and mentors at Wheaton College, former colleagues at Seattle Pacific University, and former Seattle Pacific basketball players. A personal memoir written by one of Les's sisters, Martha Habegger Schrock, provided the basis for the account of the Habegger family's earliest years in Indiana. I also relied on published sources for information about the origins of the Amish faith, the combat experience of Les Habegger's regiment in World War II, and the histories of Wheaton College and Seattle Pacific University. Press accounts covering both college and professional games in Les's coaching career augmented his near-photographic memory of pivotal contests.

I am grateful to the following people for their recollections of various aspects of Les Habegger's story: Anne Habegger, Julie Habegger, Gary Habegger, Martha Habegger Schrock, Laura Arksey, Leon Arksey, Jim Ballard, Bob Baptista, Harland Beery, Don DeHart, Frank Furtado, Sara Furtado, Fan Gates, John Glancy, Donald Horowitz, Wesley Lingren, and Bill Yeager. Talking with each of them was a true pleasure. I also appreciate the support of the Seattle Pacific University library; my thanks go especially to Robin Maass, whose assistance was invaluable.

—Doris H. Pieroth

Seattle, Washington, June 2008

ACKNOWLEDGMENTS

This book is dedicated to the people who have shaped my life, who instilled in me the characteristics that allowed me to achieve my goal of teaching young men what it means for all of us to have been created in the image of God.

To my father and mother, Jacob and Rosina Habegger, who taught me right from wrong, and who not only told me about God's love through Jesus Christ, but also lived it for all ten of us children to experience. I am also very grateful for the positive influence that the community of Berne, Indiana had on my life. After we left the Amish Church and moved to Berne, the many friends I made, along with the Sunday school teachers of the Mennonite Church, helped me to believe in a God of love rather than a God of damnation.

To my firstborn, Scott, and his sister, Julie, upon whom I showered love when they were young; and who, in their maturing years, have returned that love to me one hundred fold. Our relationship, bonded with love, reminds me again of God's unconditional love.

I was most fortunate to attend and graduate from Wheaton College in Wheaton, Illinois. I was a student there after my years in the U.S. Army and shortly after I made a commitment to Jesus Christ. I was older than most of my fellow students, but the host of friends I made accepted me and made me feel loved. I must single out one professor and his wife, Robert and Martha Baptista, in whose house I lived while I was a student. Coach Baptista and Martha were to me the epitome of love. They were like older surrogate siblings, and their wise counsel steered me down the right path.

It would be impossible to name all the colleagues and friends at Seattle Pacific that influenced my life. Given the opportunity to coach many good and talented young men in my twenty years there was a gift that God gave me. They taught me so very much, and I am eternally grateful for the relationships we had. Their influence will never leave me. They showed me that God does not live in a box, and that He manifests himself through individuals who take differing journeys and come from differing backgrounds.

I must also include the Seattle Sonics. It was an exciting time in 1977 when I was asked to become the assistant coach. To participate in the NBA championship during my first two years was more than I could have imagined. I wear that championship ring with deep gratitude to all the players who accepted me without reservation.

I owe a huge thanks to Lenny Wilkens, who included me in his preparation, planning, and game situations. He gave me the freedom to express my opinions, my ideas, and my thoughts. Never in my forty years of coaching did I have a better working relationship. I learned so much about professional basketball from Lenny, and also about life.

In the years between my eighteenth and twenty-second birthdays, I was told to leave my childhood behind and become a man instantly. During those years, I was in the U.S. Army in an infantry division, living in a foxhole on the front lines of World War II. The experience of combat is one that can only be understood by the men who were there. The men of the 70th Infantry Division, my buddies, know because they were there with me. Those who were not in the foxholes with us will not understand how love can be exhibited in a foxhole during combat, but it can, and it was. To the men of the 70th Infantry Division, I include you in my dedication of this book.

—**Les Habegger**
  Seattle, Washington
  Phoenix, Arizona

FOREWORD

The life of Les Habegger is a remarkable story of an amazing journey. He was the youngest of ten children in an Amish family in Indiana, and his early years were dominated by fear—fear of failure, damnation, and hell. Through the influence of his autocratic grandfather, who was the bishop of the local church, and the teasing Les endured as a youngster, he grew up believing he wasn't worth much and would never accomplish anything in his life. He found hope in sports, and basketball became a game that gave him encouragement and confidence.

For more than sixty years, basketball was his life. Along the way, he played and coached at the collegiate level and was a coach and manager of professional teams on two continents. Throughout his journey, he faced many career challenges in which the opportunity for success competed with the risk of failure.

Les frequently had to weigh the advice of those who said, "Don't go, you can't make it there," against the counsel of those who encouraged him to make a move. His faith sustained him as he faced the risks ahead. Often, a trusted friend met him at the intersection and pointed out the way. Always, Les was motivated by a consistent goal of helping young men lead fulfilling lives as Christians.

When Les retired, he knew that God had sustained him through his years of fear, uncertainty, and doubt. He knew he enjoyed the respect and appreciation of family, colleagues, and onlookers. Perhaps his biggest thrill came when sixty of his former players came together to honor him when he was inducted into the Seattle Pacific Athletic Hall of Fame.

This is the story of a man who has accomplished much in his lifetime. I am happy to call him my friend.

—Bob Baptista
Carol Stream, Illinois

Chapter One

SWISS ROOTS, AMERICAN BRANCHES

Amish humility and self-effacement might seem contrary to success in the fiercely competitive world of collegiate and professional basketball, but Les Habegger embodied those qualities throughout his career—from his days as a star high-school guard in the basketball hotbed of Indiana, all the way up through his tenure as general manager of a championship team in the National Basketball Association and his years in the international ranks as one of the pioneering coaches in Germany's professional *Bundesliga*.

The years spent in Germany held a natural affinity for a man who had grown up in a Swiss-German-speaking Amish family and had served in the Army of Occupation after World War II. Though as a young man he had seen the world beyond the limits of small-town Indiana, and his GI Bill benefits had taken him on to the world of higher education and to a future unimaginable to him when he was a boy, his Swiss Amish heritage defined him, and remained a controlling influence in his life.

The mention of Switzerland summons forth visions of serene Alpine meadows, vibrant centers of international finance, and precision watch-making, all served up with incomparable chocolate, cheese, fondue, and rich, dark coffee. Geneva, birthplace of the Geneva Conventions and headquarters of the International Red Cross, has long provided a beacon of hope for humanity. Their cherished neutrality insulated the Swiss from Europe's devastating wars of the twentieth century.

In the sixteenth century, however, Switzerland could not remain neutral amid the religious and political upheaval surrounding the Protestant Reformation. In 1517, Northern Europe was ripe for new religious movements when Martin Luther broke with the Roman Catholic Church and went on to create a new Lutheran Church in Germany. In neighboring Switzerland, Ulrich Zwingli and John Calvin founded the state Reformed Church, but over time, some within it wanted even more change.

Those seeking further reform were known as Anabaptists, because they rejected infant baptism, maintaining that it could not be supported by the Scriptures. They deemed un-Christian the close alliance of the Reformed church with Switzerland's political structure. In response, the state and church authorities considered Anabaptists seditious, making them subject to arrest and torture— even death or exile.

Dutch reformer Menno Simons emerged as the most important early Anabaptist leader. His followers, called Mennonites, suffered persecution and oppression, and many migrated to the Alsace region of France. Mennonites in Switzerland, Alsace, and southern Germany eventually split into two factions, primarily over disagreement about the frequency of observing Communion and on the matter of social avoidance, or "shunning," of obstinate and uncontrollable church members.

Jacob Ammann, a Swiss-born immigrant to Alsace, soon became an Anabaptist spokesman in the region. In the summer of 1693, he called for the Communion service to be observed twice a year, instead of only once, and to include ceremonial foot-washing. Perhaps more importantly, he proclaimed that nonconforming, "backsliding" members must be shunned by the faithful. He insisted on simple styles of dress for his followers, who came to be known as Amish.

At the heart of Amish beliefs is the biblical story of Creation, the Garden of Eden, and the casting out of Adam and Eve. Redemption comes by responding to the gift of God's love, a gift the Amish feel they do not deserve. Hence, they live faithfully, humbly, and gratefully in order to prove themselves worthy.

The early Amish paid heavily in blood and anguish to live in a community of like-minded believers. Repression, exile, imprisonment, and constant persecution by church and state for their nonconforming beliefs fueled an Amish migration to North America.

THE AMISH IN AMERICA

The first sizable Amish group came to Colonial America in the mid-1700s. The earliest arrivals settled primarily in Pennsylvania, but some later moved farther west into Ohio and Indiana. By the early 1840s, Swiss Amish who fled the region around Switzerland's capital city had migrated directly to Indiana's Adams County and named their new town Berne. They and their descendants continued to speak the German dialect of their Swiss homeland.

The Amish had been denied the right to hold land in Europe, but in North America these skilled farmers were free to acquire acreage and establish themselves as land owners. More essential for the Amish, conditions in Adams County gave them freedom to live a life of humility, simplicity, and love in true community, separate from the worldliness of comforts, convenience, material things, and personal enhancement.

Amish life centers on the church, but the family is basic in their stern, disciplined patriarchal society. The Amish in Adams County included a complex kinship pattern of Habeggers and Schwartzes. Jacob Ammann's inner circle in Europe had included both a Schwartz and a Habegger. Members of those two extended families played pivotal roles when the new church in Indiana endured internal conflict in 1894. The upheaval resulted in a major split in the church that had a lasting impact on the lives of succeeding generations, including that of Les Habegger.

Among the Amish, once a bishop is chosen by a congregation, he becomes its chief authority. Two preachers and a deacon complete the hierarchy. The bishop performs the rites of Communion, baptism, and marriage, as well as the excommunication and possible reinstatement of members. Les Habegger's great grandfather, Joseph Schwartz, was bishop of the Amish church in Adams County in the 1890s. When he sought full ordination for his son David as a minister in 1887, Jacob Schwartz, Joseph's brother, objected. When David's ordination was finally completed in 1888, it opened a family breach that ultimately divided the church.

David Schwartz was seen as a zealous young man who did what he considered to be right, even if it ran counter to tradition. This proved to be true around 1890, when partisan groups developed among a younger generation in the church that included some of David's siblings and cousins. He later wrote that the young dissidents had "led the bishop as they pleased," and "everything that they told him he believed to be true, even though it was false." When David corrected his father and told him how unrighteous he was to accept the dissidents' stories, the bishop became very angry. "Not only he," David said, "but also those who fed him with falsehoods began to hate me very much."

The final splintering of the church followed a bitter dispute that erupted when David Schwartz brought a "disobedient brother" before the church and called for him to be shunned. His father, the bishop, would have no part in it. The strong-willed David, convinced he was right, decided to continue the fight on principle. He assumed the matter could be settled by Amish church rules, but that didn't happen. He later said that "God did not permit them" to reconcile their differences. "He had a different plan for us. . . . God loved some of us; that is why He separated us from one another." The split occurred on June 1, 1894, and David Schwartz led his group in forming a new congregation, known as the Amish Christian Church, with himself as bishop.

Swiss Amish bishops had great authority, and Bishop David Schwartz exercised his with determination and certainty. He maintained very strict—some would say nearly tyrannical—order in his new church. Over time, he "received light from God as to what really matters," and moved his church toward a more conventional way of life than that of Old Order or "horse and buggy" Amish. Though their dress remained plain and without adornment, the men were not required to grow beards and they were allowed to cut their hair. The congregation was permitted to use some modern conveniences and drove automobiles. Even so, Bishop David Schwartz ruled his church with an iron hand worthy of an Old World despot.

In 1883, David Schwartz had married the "devout and God fearing" Anna Steury. Together they had ten children, the fourth of whom—a daughter named Rosina—was born April 4, 1890. On August 7, 1910, Rosina Schwartz married Jacob Habegger, whose family had come to America in 1865 and settled in Adams County, Indiana. Rosina and Jacob Habegger had ten children of their own—four girls and six boys born within a twelve year span. Their youngest child, born November 13, 1924, they named Lester Noah Habegger.

CHAPTER TWO

FAMILY TIES

There is no end to theories about how birth order in a family significantly influences a child's development and determines personality. When Les Habegger's siblings would tease him about being the baby of the family—as they often did—he would say, "It took Mom and Dad ten tries to get perfection." But as the youngest of ten, he grew up thinking that his family considered him a baby, always treated him as a baby, and thought him worthless and not likely to accomplish much.

The Habeggers' family life centered on the Amish Christian Church of Bishop David Schwartz, and their grandfather's inflexible rule dominated every aspect of their lives. Fear of damnation from his grandfather, and the notion of insignificance and inferiority he got from his brothers and sisters, filled Les's formative years. He never completely overcame those feelings, even when success and acclaim later came to him.

The three oldest of Jacob and Rosina Habegger's children were sisters Selma, Martha, and Metta, who were born in Berne, Indiana. They were joined by brother Joel following the family's move to a small farm north of town. They moved again in 1916 to rent the eighty-acre Isadore Kalver farm, three miles south of Monroe, the county seat, and the other six children were born there. Rosina and Jacob favored biblical names for their sons—Joel, Eli, David, and Jesse—until they reached the final two, Clifton and Lester.

Jacob worked as a sharecropper, and Les's overriding memory of his childhood was one of deprivation and of the family being incredibly poor. His sister Martha agreed, saying, "There was never any money for pleasure. Dad or Mother went to town no more than once or twice a month, and there was a sort of lottery (sometimes according to past behavior, sometimes according to age) to see who could go along. That was an incentive to be good." When an itinerant peddler visited the farm between those trips to town, Rosina bought staples, or bartered with eggs, cream, fresh vegetables, and chickens. Martha remembered that "once in a while we had enough to barter for wieners or bananas. What a treat that was!"

The economic recession that dogged the agriculture heartland during the 1920s turned into the Great Depression. In 1929, the First Bank of Decatur foreclosed on the Kalvers' farm mortgage, forcing the Habeggers to move once again. They settled on the Simon Sprunger farm, two and half miles north of Berne. Les was five years old at the time, and his memories of childhood center mainly on life on the Sprunger farm. Eight of the children were then going to school, and every fall they lacked ready money for books and shoes. Martha said their father sometimes had to sell chickens, heifers, or grain to get money for school supplies.

HELLFIRE AND FEAR

Through all their moves, the family maintained their connection to the Amish Christian Church. Bishop David Schwartz continued the twice-yearly observance of Communion, complete with the foot-washing ritual, and the basic Amish discipline of shunning the apostate. But hellfire was the bishop's fundamental message, and that was the picture of God that Les Habegger absorbed. "Never, ever did I hear the word *love* in that church—it was God's judgment, God's condemnation, God's wrath." His grandfather preached that behavior determined salvation, "and the word *grace* was not even part of his language."

Bishop Schwartz held overwhelming power and influence over the entire congregation—adults and children alike. He controlled every aspect of their lives; no one dared make a move without his permission. His rule was one of fear and condemnation. The Habegger children were taught to believe their grandfather was "God's man" and that he could do no wrong. Martha was "deathly afraid of him," and the dominant emotion of Les's childhood was "fear, fear, fear, fear, fear."

As Les put it, "Grandpa *was* the church. Whatever Grandpa said, that was it—he spoke ex cathedra." They were taught that the bishop's power came from God, that his church was the only church, and that anybody who was not a member of his church was lost. "If you didn't belong to his church, you were going to hell."

Members of the church were not allowed to darken the door of another congregation. When Les was eight years old, his grandfather asked him, "How do you know you're going to get to heaven?"

"If I obey you, Grandpa," Les remembers saying. And that was the right answer.

Decades later, in his mind's eye, he could still see his grandfather standing in front of the congregation and calling out names of members of the church as part of his sermon about their behavior. Reports such as, "This week somebody saw you on the streets of Berne, and you were laughing," were sufficient for him to condemn a member publicly. In some cases, the bishop considered a person's behavior or lifestyle abhorrent enough to excommunicate the offender. Family members were not immune if they "didn't follow what Grandpa said." He excommunicated two of his own sons. Les recalled that when those two uncles visited his home, Rosina wouldn't let them in the house. "They had to stay on the porch, and eat on the porch, because they couldn't associate with members of the church when they were excommunicated."

Adults as well as children were "scared stiff of Grandpa Schwartz," Martha recalled. Her parents "wouldn't do anything without asking him if it was okay. If Dad cut hay and it rained on it, and he hadn't asked Grandpa, or if he sold hogs and the price went up or down," he knew he would be chastised for it.

The older Habegger siblings lived almost as indentured servants. Martha said that her life as a teenager was so restricted that "there was no pleasure in living." Although Bishop Schwartz allowed automobiles, he was very strict about things he considered worldly. "We were not allowed to have connections with anyone outside his church," Martha said. "No theater, no dancing, no entertainment of any kind." Dress was plain. Colors could not be bright. Skirts had to be a certain length, and a woman's hair had to be worn in a certain style." Jacob would occasionally rearrange the girls' hair into a more acceptable style. "Above all, we were allowed absolutely no makeup," said Martha. "Lipstick came from the devil! I did pinch my cheeks, though, to make them look red."

Les's lasting memory of the bishop was that when he came to the farm, it was always to criticize. Whenever the kids saw his car approaching the house along the lane from the main road, they would whisper, "Oh no, here comes Grandpa," and be absolutely scared to pieces, because they knew something had gone wrong. "And my poor mother—his daughter," Les said. "Grandpa just was so negative, and judgmental, and critical. If he came, it was to scold, not to visit."

TIGHT TIMES DURING THE DEPRESSION

Bishop Schwartz had virtually dictated the family's relocation when the Habeggers had to move from the Kalver farm in 1929. He instructed his brother-in-law, a church member, to buy a farm so Rosina and her family could move. The brother-in-law didn't need or want another farm, but the power of the bishop prevailed, and he bought the Sprunger farm three miles away. Les's eldest brother, Joel, at the age of fourteen, was sent to work as a hired hand for the owner of the newly purchased farm, and he worked for free to pay the rent for the farm.

All the Habegger children contributed to the family coffers. Their parents did the best they knew how under the circumstances, but when the children were sixteen years old, and had thus met the state's minimum education requirements, they went to work. In September 1929, Jacob Habegger obtained a work permit from the county superintendent so Martha would not have to start school that fall. She had begun working at a garment factory in Berne in May, but when jobs became scarce as the Depression deepened, she did mostly housework. All the money she earned was turned over to her father. "I made two dollars a week," she said, "working twelve miles from home. My father took me on Monday morning and came after me on Friday evening—and I politely handed the two dollars over to him. We didn't know any different."

All the Habegger kids were "farmed out." When Les was twelve or thirteen, he too went to work for a neighbor and turned his seventy-five-cent daily wage over to his father.

None of the children spoke English until they went to school. Les remembered once speaking English after school and having his father tell him, "In my house, we speak German." So they all spoke German, with a Swiss dialect. The language issue caused young Les some discomfort on trips into town with his mother. "Before we would go, I would beg her, 'Mom, when we get in the stores, please don't talk German,' because I was embarrassed."

Jacob Habegger conducted his family's daily devotions in German and read aloud from the family Bible with its well-worn leather cover. He said grace both before and after every meal, and the children could not leave the table until he dismissed them. At night, Jacob also read from the Bible, but that was less memorable for Les than his prayers. "We all had to kneel down, and Dad prayed before we could go to bed. I can still see the living room. Everybody had to kneel down—the whole family. All of us kids who were at home. At times, some of us would fall sleep as he prayed forever, and we'd have to be awakened after he was through, to send us off to bed."

Les may well have gone to bed with images left in his head from the nightly Bible reading. The richly illustrated German Bible contained lavish color depictions of biblical characters and events, such as scenes from Genesis—the Creation, the Fall, and the Expulsion from the Garden. But given the negative, hellfire and damnation message he received from his grandfather, it was the drawings of hell that had the greatest impact on Les. He thought the artist's renditions were real pictures of what hell looked like, especially one "where God was throwing people into hell." Decades later, he said the scenes were "as vivid to me now as they were then. Dark valleys filled with seas of flames in which those poor lost souls were drowning in fire . . . holding their hands up in the air as if begging to escape or reaching for salvation."

The Habeggers' two-story frame house, a typical 1920s Midwest farmhouse, was drafty in the winter, stiflingly hot in the summer, and would have benefited from a fresh coat of paint. A welcoming front porch, complete with a swing, provided cool relief for visitors and family alike on hot, humid summer evenings. With the eldest son, Joel, living away, the four bedrooms accommodated the remaining nine children and their parents. The four girls shared one room and brothers Eli and David another. The youngest boys—Les, Cliff, and Jess—shared a third room and the same bed.

The farmhouse had no furnace. A coal stove in the dining room heated the whole house. Les recalled that his father rose early, at 4:00 or 4:30, to stoke the stove so that when everyone else got up, it was nice and hot. Les and his brothers and sisters would run downstairs in the morning and dress in front of the stove. "We were all there dressing together," he said.

On one particularly cold Indiana winter morning, when Les looked into the open door of the stove, the flames reminded him of the family Bible's depiction of hell.

"It's hard to convey the feeling of fear that was driven into me as a little boy," Les said. "The fact that you're going to hell, and that it's a place where it's hot, and there's fire. I remember thinking, *Is hell this hot, or is it hotter?* as I looked into that little stove—the hot coals, the red embers in there. Grandpa always preached that we would burn forever, so I thought about that, and the word *forever* became a terrible word for me. I remember standing by the stove thinking, *How long is forever?*"

The indelible mark of his grandfather's power and authority remained with Les his entire life. "To this day, I still have memories that haunt me."

LIFE ON THE FARM

The Habeggers' farmhouse had neither electricity nor running water, which was standard for the day. With no indoor plumbing, the family would run out back to the outhouse during the day. At night, it was a different story. In most homes, the lack of plumbing meant having a basin, pitcher, and "slop jar" in every bedroom. Jacob Habegger provided a big bucket in the middle of the upstairs hallway for the entire family to use, and it filled up quickly.

The bed that Les shared with two of his brothers had no conventional mattress. With money scarce, Rosina had sewn a mattress cover from a heavy, denim-like fabric, and Jacob had stuffed it with corn husks. As the three boys turned and tossed around in their sleep, the husks would work their way out from the center, leaving the boys piled together in the middle. With six boys in the family, the law of averages almost mandated that one of them would suffer the bane of young boys—bed-wetting. This did not bode well for the corn husk mattress or the bed's other occupants. House rules dictated that the last user of the bucket had to empty it first thing in the morning. To avoid that loathsome chore, the boys were not above simply utilizing an open window instead of the bucket to meet their nightly needs.

Other chores they could not so easily escape. Lack of running water meant bathing once a week in a tub that Rosina washed clothes in. Les's brothers and sisters may have been convinced that he was babied and "got away with murder," but as the youngest, his turn in the bathtub was last, by which time the well-used water was barely lukewarm. At laundry time, the boys filled the tub in the basement by hand from the well in the yard. Les eventually inherited this chore from his brothers. He also took the clean laundry out to hang on the clothesline with wooden pins. Sometimes, a big summertime thunderstorm would come up and he'd have to run out and gather the clothes before they were soaked again. In winter, the laundry hung on lines in the basement where the temperature often fell below freezing, turning sheets and shirts into stiff objects that would crack if not handled carefully.

For a long time, Rosina did the entire family laundry by hand on a wood-framed corrugated steel wash board. Emptying and refilling the tub with rinse water was part of Les's responsibility. His mother repeatedly scrubbed each item against the board, which was submerged in soapy water, and she surely sacrificed skin from her knuckles in the process. Each piece also required hand wringing. The Habeggers later acquired a washing machine with a hand-cranked wringer that made laundry something of a team sport. Les would feed the clothes between the wringer's two rollers or catch them as they came through ready to be hung on the line.

Les's summer chores included making sure to get the cows out of the pasture and into the barn in time so his father and brothers could milk them. His mother's kitchen had a wood-burning cook stove, and he was responsible for keeping it supplied with wood from the woodshed located a slight distance from the house. When Les was very young, the notorious gangster John Dillinger was roaming the upper Midwest, robbing banks and terrifying the countryside. For an anxious and frightened little boy, this was enough to make him balk at bringing in the wood. Les recalled telling his parents, "I don't want to go out there. John Dillinger might be out there in the shed!"

Fear of gangsters did not prevent Les from keeping his mother supplied with wood for the stove on which she produced her savory stews, roasts, chicken dishes, and his favorite apple dumplings. Fresh vegetables and berries from the garden, eggs from the hens, ham and bacon from the hogs, and milk and cream from their cows kept all the Habeggers well fed. As Les recalled, "We had no money, we were poor, but we never went hungry, because we lived on the farm."

Nor did they go thirsty. Their Swiss heritage included a taste for wine and beer. The basement of the farmhouse served as Jacob's brewery and wine cellar, and his home brew was the standard drink at mealtime for all ages in the family, including young Les.

Bishop Schwartz did not rail against wine and beer, which figured significantly in one of the community's few seasonal celebrations. Near midnight on December 31, all the adults would progress from house to house, singing a traditional German song of good wishes for the coming year. The welcome at each stop included free-flowing spirits. Les well remembered that the revelers, after several stops and drinking wine, were "very merry" and had a happy new year, "but that, according to Grandpa, was not evil. He loved his wine and beer."

Les did attest, however, to the Bishop's prohibition of Christmas celebrations. "Grandpa took the biblical admonition that we are 'in the world but not of the world' literally. In this case, it meant no 'worldly' celebration; no presents, no Christmas tree, no decorations. In other words, what 'the world' did, we didn't."

Christmas was strictly a religious holiday, but one memorable year, Jacob bought a sack of oranges, placed it on the kitchen table and told Rosina and the kids, "This is a present for the family." Les does not remember feeling sad as a little boy that the family didn't have a traditional Christmas with presents. "We were so indoctrinated that it was evil that we didn't think any other way."

During the school year, the Habegger clan would be up by 6:30, have breakfast, and then leave for school. They walked the three miles to the Amish Christian Church's parochial school, an eight-grade, one-room school that served thirty or so children from the congregation. With a Schwartz uncle in charge, the school was ingrained with Grandfather Schwartz's rules. For Les, fear was the dominant emotion.

A curtain divided the lower grades from the sixth, seventh, and eighth graders, but Les remembers that it offered scant privacy. "Just about every morning, we'd see that curtain go up and we'd say, 'Uh-oh, now comes a lecture from Uncle Jack.' You knew that someone was about to get chewed out in front of the whole school. One guy was taken to task because he parted his hair in the middle."

After school, the Habegger clan made the three-mile trek back to the farm to take on the afternoon's chores.

THE BISHOP FALLS

Amish youth were forbidden to go on to high school, but in 1933, a series of events began that would completely change Les Habegger's future, including his educational opportunities. That year, his grandfather's power and authority came under severe scrutiny, doubt, and questioning, which eventually undermined his hold over the congregation.

No one could have foreseen that some family wedding plans would have such far-reaching effects. It all began when Les's sister Martha became engaged to marry Noah Schrock.

> With Grandpa . . . in complete control, we had to get permission from him. All was well, and we planned a double wedding, with my sister Selma and [her fiancé] Amos Inniger, to take place on March 6, 1933. Grandma became ill, and about a week before this date she died. We had to postpone the wedding because Grandpa was so grief stricken. We should not have any joy either. . . . We tried to set another date, but we were not allowed to get married until he found another wife. To our disbelief, he had someone within two months. Now we were to have a triple wedding.

The triple wedding took place on May 14. One church historian reported that, to help the girls' family, the congregation furnished a carry-in dinner in the church basement. "One can envision a happy and cozy atmosphere, with the seventy-one-year-old grandfather and two of his granddaughters enjoying a wedding meal together."

The bishop's second marriage lasted just over two years—until his wife, Elizabeth, died of a heart attack while working in the berry patch. The family's disbelief that had accompanied his hurried remarriage in 1933 turned to anger and indignation. As Martha later wrote, "He immediately wanted another wife, but this time [the family] objected to his behavior, and interfered." The church had held together the first time around, "but then it popped open like a balloon . . . [as] his followers were finally convinced that he wasn't the Man of God he had everyone believing . . . and no one trusted him anymore."

In May 1936, the bishop was excommunicated from the church, on the grounds of "moral misconduct." David Schwartz gave his own account of the events: "I was removed from the ministerial office . . . [and] placed in the ban, all out of envy and spite."

Following his expulsion as bishop, David Schwartz moved into the home of his eldest daughter, Susan, Mrs. Jacob Liechty, in Fort Wayne, Indiana. As Les recalled, "The Liechtys had sided in with him, and for a long time after the church breakup, Mother and her sister didn't talk, and we didn't associate with our cousins. Later on, we did see the bishop occasionally, but not very often. I didn't like him." His grandfather had permanently marked his childhood with negativity and left him with an ingrained fear of God and hellfire.

In the wake of the upheaval, members left the Amish Christian Church and joined other congregations. Noah and Martha Schrock, the young newlyweds, were among the first to leave. They joined the First Mennonite Church in Berne. Les and his family also left, but they did not affiliate elsewhere until he and one of his brothers began attending the Mennonite Church.

Les had once told one of his Mennonite neighbors, who was his own age, "Doris, you're going to hell . . . because you don't belong to our church." Bishop Schwartz had taught his congregation to believe that anyone who didn't belong to his church was going to hell; and members were not allowed—ever—to enter the door of another church, because that was "wrong." When Les and his family left the bishop's church, Doris urged him to come to hers. At some point, his parents said, "Okay, you can go," and one Sunday he and Cliff went with Doris to the Mennonite church.

Having been taught that if he stepped into another church it was going to burn down, Les remembers thinking when he walked into the Mennonite building, "Uh-oh, the chandeliers are going to fall down, or something." But the chandeliers did not crash, Jacob and Rosina eventually joined their sons at the Mennonite church, and they later became members.

FEELING INFERIOR

Although Les was the youngest, he occasionally gave as good as he got with his siblings. For the most part, however, from his own perspective, he was picked on and treated as the baby. He grew up with a real sense that he wasn't going to do anything of consequence; that he wasn't going to amount to very much. From his father, he got the message that the family's dire economic straits meant they were socially inferior and could not do what others did. He recalled his father saying, "Others can, but we can't," and this contributed to his feeling that he wasn't worth very much.

The way his brothers and sisters reacted to a harrowing episode when he was ten years old did nothing to strengthen his self-esteem. In looking back, he said, "It found its way into my psyche." His sister Martha recalled that Les was sick for three days with what their mother thought was the stomach flu, but when his condition worsened and he ran a high fever, the local doctor said he had to be taken to the hospital. This created a dilemma for his parents, who had no health insurance and no money. The doctor insisted that the county would pay for it, and he drove Les to the Decatur hospital himself.

Upon closer examination, they discovered that Les's appendix had ruptured, perhaps three days earlier, and gangrene had developed. In the pre-wonder drug days of 1934, this was a grave diagnosis. They did not remove the appendix, but the area was

19

cleaned and tubes were inserted for drainage. The doctors told the family, "He won't live 36 hours."

Martha recalled that, in view of such a grim prospect, when Les asked for ice cream, the doctor said to give him anything he wanted. "His room was open, and the family and friends went in and out as we pleased—no restrictions." Les never forgot hearing a sibling say, "Well, they just sewed him back up because the doctor said he's going to die. Give him two or three days and he'll be dead."

After the third day, however, when Les showed signs of improvement, they closed his door, cutting off the steady stream of visitors—except immediate family—and nixed the ice cream. No one could believe the remarkable turnaround.

Les recalled that, after he returned home, his brothers would point out a place in the house and say, "Yeah, we were going to have your casket right over there." Visiting relatives told him, "We thought you were going to die." Rosina saw his recovery as an answer to prayer. Les himself said he survived "only by the grace of God."

Though their childhood had its somber and negative aspects and lacked material things, Martha recalled, "We had some good times too, for at that time there were enough of us to form a baseball or a basketball team (when we had time to play). Ten children, twelve years apart, brought about many squabbles, but we all survived."

Les agreed. "We never bought anything, but we created our own games, and we played games in the house—all of us kids. And we had fun."

The farmhouse had a large living room, but the dining room was where they typically played. One favorite indoor game was blind mice, for which they pushed the dining room table and chairs up against the walls and blindfolded one child who would try to catch everybody. "And of course we're running here and there, and running into each other," Les recalled.

At other, calmer, times, they marked a circle with chalk on the linoleum floor and played marbles. "After virtually every shot," Les said, "there would be big fights—whether you hit the marble in the circle, or you didn't. And, of course, then Dad would come in and get us."

Somewhat surprisingly, in those days, card playing was okay, so the kids played cards. "And that was another time when we'd fight, and then Dad would come and take the pack of cards." Asked whether his father was the one who kept order, Les emphatically said, "You better believe it."

For outdoor fun, the Habeggers and their neighboring friends congregated in the summertime and played games such as hide and seek. "And then, of course, basketball was a big deal," Les said.

HABEGGER HOOPS

Les cannot remember life without basketball. The area near the entrance to the barn was equipped with a metal barrel hoop that served as an indoor basket, and they nailed another hoop outside on the hog shed for use in the summertime. "From the time I can remember," Les said, "sports was a part of our activity. And we played basketball."

He played basketball inside the house, as well. "Mother made a little ball, about the size of a baseball, out of rags, and I would take that and I would play inside the house, up against the wall—imagining there was a basket." He shot imaginary baskets by the hour.

The boys' first official basketball for outdoor use probably belonged in a museum, even before they acquired it. A scarred leather cover enclosed a rubber bladder, which they inflated with a hand pump. Les recalled that the bladder would burst—"and then we'd have to patch it up some way." He had no idea where it came from, "But I know it didn't cost very much, or we'd have never had it."

When Jacob and Rosina Habegger left the Amish Christian Church, their children left the parochial school, as well. The public school was an eight-grade, red brick structure in Monroe Township. When Les and Cliff reached the seventh and eighth grades, a young teacher named Howard Brandberry arrived. The boys still felt some uncertainty and a void in their lives in the wake of their grandfather's removal from the center of everything. Brandberry connected with them by plugging into their one great passion: basketball. He set up a backboard and basket of official dimensions in the schoolyard where the boys played.

There was an annual Adams County junior high basketball tournament for all the schools in the county, and Brandberry entered the Monroe Township school in the tournament. Les, Cliff, and one of their cousins were three of the six players on the team. "That's all we had," Les said. "Six guys. We entered the tournament, and we won it." His basketball career was off to a good start.

Rosina Habegger saw to it that her sons had identifying uniforms for that first tournament. She bought felt yard goods and cut, stitched, and transformed their sleeveless undershirts—which was standard team garb—with the letters "Monroe TWP." Les had no idea where she got the money, "but she got enough to make the letters, so we had Monroe Township on our uniforms."

Howard Brandberry was the first person beyond family to have any real influence in Les Habegger's life. Les remembered him as "a good guy," and recalled the summer when Brandberry underwrote a week's vacation at a nearby lake for a group of boys from Monroe. He also made it possible for Les and Cliff to go to a movie at the theater in Decatur. They told him, "We're not allowed to go . . . it's forbidden. We're not even allowed to go into a theater." So Brandberry went to talk with their parents; it was a watershed moment.

"He sat down with Mom and Dad and explained to them what this movie was about. It was a Western, *The Bad Man of Brimstone*, with Wallace Beery. I'll never forget it. He explained to my folks, 'This is a cowboy movie. There's nothing bad about it.' I don't know how, but they let us go, and that was the first movie we got to see—and that would have been in 1937 or '38."

A long-standing edict of the Amish Christian Church had been that no one attended movies, high school athletic contests, plays, or musical concerts. Les was amazed that his parents were willing to support basketball, the kids' other activities, and that they allowed an occasional freedom. "There was no frivolity in my dad's life. You just stayed to the theme. And he himself didn't ever do anything, but somehow he let the reins go, and let us go ahead and play. I think Mom had a great influence on Dad."

His parents went to the games "once in a while," when he and Cliff played in high school. They were both very good players, at the high school in Berne, after the family moved to town. Les remembered the games they attended, and he was certain that "Mom was instrumental in bringing Dad there."

His freshman year was spent at the high school in Monroe, while they were still on the farm, but they moved into the town of Berne in the fall of 1940. Jacob went to work at the town's furniture factory, as did Les's brothers. Les himself worked at the factory on summer vacations during his high school years. His father built frames for the upholstered furniture, and Les's job was tying springs. He also did some upholstery—"actually putting the cloth on."

Living in town, there was a bit more freedom for the Habeggers. (The ban on moviegoing had been lifted, so once in a great while they saw a film. But they had to drive to Monroe, because Berne had no theater of its own.) But there was no compromising of the work ethic. Les said, "We worked. I'd shovel the neighbors' snow in the winter. Made a little money shoveling sidewalks. Some had paper routes. We didn't have any money to do a lot of things."

He went to school, he worked, and he played basketball. The school day ended at three o'clock, followed by basketball practice that lasted until five-thirty. Then they would go home, have dinner, and do the chores. Les did not remember having much homework.

When asked later what his favorite high school subject had been, he laughed and said, "Basketball. I was not a very good student. I was not very good in math and science, because I didn't want to work that hard. I was lazy. I wanted to play ball, so I kept my grades up. But I have to be honest—I was lazy." He also took German, which was an obvious elective for a boy raised in a Swiss Amish home. He later became an avid reader, but not when he was in high school. "Back then, I was a player, not a reader."

LEARNING SOME LESSONS

At Berne High School, Les encountered two more people who would influence his life: Lake Glendenning, Berne's basketball coach during his sophomore and junior years; and Carolyn Hershey, the school principal. He remembered Principal Hershey as "a wonderful lady," and said that Glendenning "was very instrumental in my development in high school—and we kept in touch."

Lake Glendenning was "just a really nice guy" in the competitive atmosphere of Indiana high school basketball. Berne was a small town, and everyone supported the team. Les said, "If your house caught fire during a ballgame, it was going to burn down, because everybody was at the game."

The pressure to win was also strong. "In Indiana, you played basketball, and if you didn't win . . ."

But Glendenning always treated his players with respect and kindness. "He was a good coach. We won, we had good teams." Les did not recall any tirades or noteworthy disciplinary drills when they lost. Positive reinforcement marked Glendenning's approach to coaching, and his players admired him tremendously.

One memorable loss for Berne came in Indiana's single-class state tournament, which concluded each basketball season. In Indiana's unique system—captured most memorably in the movie *Hoosiers*— the small-town schools would play the largest schools from Fort Wayne or Indianapolis. The initial, or sectional, round was played within each county, and the brackets were set by luck of the draw.

When Les was a junior, Berne and Monroe had the two best teams in Adams County. As luck would have it, Berne drew Monroe in the first round. In that era, the high schools played thirty-two minute games—eight minute quarters. Decades later, Les vividly recalled that game's crucial minutes.

"We were behind at halftime. We were behind by sixteen points in the third quarter. Cliff and I started to press—we were the guards, and we started to press—and we ended up winning the game. We beat Monroe 41-40. I still remember the score."

With their top local rival now out of the tournament, Berne moved on to the second round to face Pleasant Mills, a team from a consolidated school out in the country. "They were not a good team," Les recalled. "We had a very good team, so we're thinking we're already going to win the sectional and move on. Pleasant Mills beat us, 28-26. I'll never forget it."

After paying the price for overconfidence and looking beyond their opponent, the team sat dejected in the locker room. "Everybody was just devastated, because we thought we had the sectional. The coach was as devastated as we were. His wife even came into the locker room crying. So, we're sitting there, and suddenly the door of the locker room opened up and in walked our physics teacher—a six-foot four-inch redhead named Bill Spurgeon. I'll never forget it. We're all sitting there, just beside ourselves, and he stands there, and he looks at us, and he says, 'You people should be ashamed of yourself, sitting here crying over a basketball game, and today Singapore fell.'"

In February 1942, the name Singapore meant little in small-town Indiana. As Les remembered it, "All of us there were wondering, 'Singapore, let's see . . . who did they play? Who are they?' We hadn't the foggiest idea what Mr. Spurgeon was talking about."

Their physics teacher had tried to put things into perspective for them with little success. But the team would soon learn the significance of the fall of Singapore in World War II—and the growing war would soon take its toll on Les and his teammates. The first blow came when Coach Glendenning was drafted at the beginning of Les's senior year. "So we got somebody else who was a disaster in our senior year."

Before the age of television, the average fifteen-year-old was much less aware of world affairs than are teenagers growing up today on a twenty-four-hour news cycle. Jacob Habegger subscribed to a local publication, the Berne *Witness*, whose front page proudly proclaimed it as "Indiana's only Tri-Weekly Newspaper." To get a newspaper from Indianapolis or Fort Wayne, they could go down to the drugstore and buy it, but it was certainly not delivered to the house. Once Les was allowed to go to the movies, he might have learned from the accompanying newsreels that Japan had invaded China in 1937; and he would have seen evidence of the German rearmament and Nazi aggression. But it all seemed so remote in isolationist Indiana, especially among the pacifistic Amish community.

Jacob Habegger had ordered a radio from the Spiegel catalog in 1938, and he followed the news of impending war in Europe very closely. Les remembered his father sitting by the radio one evening in late summer 1939, listening intently to a news program. Jacob said to himself in German, not knowing Les was in earshot, "Now we're going to have war; now we're going to have war." As a pacifist who remembered what was then known as the Great War, Jacob was understandably concerned. "There's going to be a war. I know it.

We can't be a part of this. We can't go off and kill people." It all still seemed so improbable.

The United States had begun its own mobilization in 1940, enlarging the navy, strengthening the air force, launching the Lend Lease" program to bolster Great Britain and Russia, and instating a military draft. But not until December 7, 1941, did the reality of the war begin to hit home for Les and most other Americans. Even then, it took a while for him to fully comprehend it.

On that "day that will live in infamy," Les was doing what any athletic Indiana boy would do on a beautiful December weekend. He was shooting baskets. The backboard was in the driveway of his friend Jim McCorrick, who lived just a block or two from the Habeggers.

"We were out there shooting baskets," Les recalled, "and Jim said, 'Did you hear that Pearl Harbor was bombed?' And I said, 'No, where's Pearl Harbor?' He says, 'Well, it's over in Hawaii.' 'Yeah?— well who bombed it?' He said, 'The Japanese.' And I remember saying, 'That's going to be a war of about two weeks.' That was all that was said."

When Les went home and reflected on things, he thought, *Okay, but it's not going to affect me. My brothers, yeah, but not me.* "I was seventeen years old, so it was just, 'Yeah, no big deal.' We were in Indiana. There was no danger of anything." He never thought it would have any impact on his life.

But in a very short time, even Indiana, where danger seemed remote, was on a wartime footing. Young men began to leave Berne for military induction centers, and the town welcomed them back in uniform when they came home on leave. By the summer of 1943, four of Les's brothers had either enlisted or been drafted into the service. When the Amish Christian Church broke apart in 1936, Joel had left the farm where he had worked and had gone to high school, and then on to the Ohio State University, where he was a member of the Army ROTC. He was soon called to active duty. Dave, too, went into the army, while Jess and Cliff served in the Army Air Corps. Their parents found all this difficult to accept.

Les celebrated his eighteenth birthday in November 1942, and registered for the draft. His induction notice arrived the following March. He received a deferment in order to graduate from high school, but in July 1943, he too left for the army. His father was more strongly opposed to Les's enlistment than his mother was, because she was firmly convinced he would never pass the army's physical examination. Rosina was certain that Les's weakened health, following his brush with death in the appendix episode, would keep him safe.

Les took the one-day physical at Camp Perry, near Toledo, Ohio, on July 29, 1943. When he returned home, his mother and father were sitting in the porch swing waiting for him. As he walked up the steps, he laughed and told them he had passed. His mother would not believe it.

"You did not," she said.

"Yes—I—did." Les replied.

Rosina was devastated. "I was happy; she was devastated. Her youngest, her baby, and I was—in her mind, there was no way I could have passed the physical."

Her state of mind was not helped by a Mennonite church friend who commented on her now having five sons in the service: "Oh, Mrs. Habegger, it would be too much to ask God to bring them all back."

CHAPTER THREE

BREAKING AWAY

The core Amish values of obedience, humility, and simplicity all run counter to the use of force. As with the Mennonites and Quakers, the Amish do not participate in military service. During the twentieth century, most young men from these faiths claimed conscientious objector status when faced with conscription. World War I had seen COs drafted into the army, but with no alternative service planned by the government, they were sent to army camps where they frequently found themselves languishing in solitary confinement, experiencing physical abuse, or facing court martial. The "war to end all wars" had virtually unanimous, nationwide patriotic backing. That support had eventually taken an ugly turn toward nativism and bigotry. Military intelligence had kept the Mennonites and Amish under surveillance during the entire war.

With the painful and shocking experiences of the World War I conscientious objectors fully in mind, leaders of the three historic peace churches took steps to prevent the problem from recurring as the Second World War approached. The Nazi regime in Germany presented a clear-cut case of good versus evil—a fight against tyranny.

They worked to create a program of alternative service that would give conscientious objectors opportunities to do humanitarian work instead of serving in the military or being jailed. The 1940 Draft Act contained an alternative service clause that reflected these efforts by acknowledging a class of COs that would do work of national importance under civilian supervision.

The program that grew out of this initiative was known as Civilian Public Service, jointly administered by the U.S. government and a church agency. Men in the CPS worked in hospitals, or in such areas as forestry and soil conservation. Jacob Habegger fervently wanted such a posting for his youngest son.

Rosina's brother David, son of the former bishop, had been drafted into the army in World War I, and another member of Berne's Amish Christian Church had spent two years of the war in the federal prison at Fort Leavenworth. Jacob must surely have had their experiences in mind when Les returned triumphantly after taking his army physical. Both parents reacted in disbelief when he told them he had passed. Les said his father was shocked, "but Mom did more of the talking, as mothers do." When he finally spoke, Jacob said, "Well, you're going to sign up as a conscientious objector."

Les responded by saying, "I'm not going to do that, Dad. I'm not going to walk down the streets of this town and have people say I'm a draft dodger. I'm not going to do it."

Young Amish men did not defy their fathers. "For me in particular," Les said, "having been raised in an anti-political home— in the world but not of it—it was really quite something." After Les had forcefully presented his case against claiming conscientious objector status, Jacob said, "Okay, you're going to sign up as a noncombatant. If you don't want to be a conscientious objector then you can sign in as a noncombatant."

Classification 1-AO meant you were physically fit to serve, but as one who did not carry arms. Les signed up as a noncombatant," because my father said that's what you do."

Preparing for War

It can be argued that in keeping their young men from military service, the Amish elders had sought to protect them from worldly influences. Once he had chosen to go into the army, Les Habegger would encounter virtually every influence of the wider world and every temptation known to man.

Like most American small towns in 1943, Berne, Indiana, kept track of its servicemen. Three times a week, the Berne *Witness* printed the names of those who were leaving. In their front windows, families proudly displayed flags with a blue star emblem for each son or husband in the service. Jacob and Rosina Habegger's flag had five blue stars.

Les and his friends Ron and Gaylord left on August 19. "People were leaving every day," he said. "After the class of '43 graduated, we were all gone."

They had no big send-off. His sister Rose drove him and his friends to Decatur to board a bus full of young men from all over Adams County, bound for the induction center at Fort Benjamin Harrison in Indianapolis.

Les reported as a noncombatant, took the oath, and received a uniform. At the fort, men were assigned to specific camps in various parts of the country, and to a designated branch—artillery, engineering, ordinance, infantry, and so on. Les was assigned to the 274th Regiment Medical Detachment of the 70th Infantry Division.

A noncombatant's assignment could be anything—such as clerical support—where he would not be on the front lines carrying a rifle. Most noncombatants went into the medical corps, where they might work in a hospital or as medics assigned to combat units. Les said, "Hospitals, obviously, are way back from the front lines, but I'm certain my father didn't know that the infantry that were up there in the foxholes needed medics more than anybody else."

The 70th Infantry Division, known as the Trailblazers, was sent to Camp Adair, Oregon, at the end of August. Of the 150 medics in his detachment, Les estimated that there were only about four who were actual noncombatants. The rest, just by the luck of the draw, got put into the medics. One of his colleagues joked that the army had made him a medic because, as a civilian, he had worked for Dr. Pepper.

During their thirteen weeks of basic training, the medics did a lot of marching and calisthenics, but did no formal training with rifles or hand grenades. They did, however, fire on the rifle range, even though they would not be furnished weapons for combat. Jacob believed that noncombatant status would keep Les from harm's way; but what it actually did was send him into harm's way without his own rifle to defend himself. "My father never knew any of this, of course, but when you're an aid man with a rifle company, which I was, you're in a foxhole with another soldier, sometimes for several days. When the infantryman slept, I took the rifle and stood guard."

He spent the rest of his time in Oregon in advanced training as a medic. The focus was on rudimentary first aid and training for emergencies. "The aid man's job was simply to stop the bleeding— to keep the wounded man alive. In those days, tourniquets were used, and the first thing we learned to do was give a morphine shot. And they'd teach you how to bandage. For example, how do you bandage a head wound? That was pretty much it."

By 1943, the new sulfa "wonder drugs" were available. "Sulfa powder and sulfa pills are what we had. So you'd throw the sulfa into a wound and bandage it up." The equipment he carried included two medical pouches full of dressings, scissors, morphine, and sulfa.

In the rich and fertile Willamette Valley, Camp Adair claimed 65,000 acres just north of Corvallis. A history of the regiment says that when they converted farmland into an army base with some 1,700 wooden buildings, 250 of the "most productive farms in the state, many owned by families of nineteenth-century pioneers" were sacrificed to the cause. Camp Adair lay on the river's west bank, with the mountains of the Coast Range between it and the Siuslaw National Forest and one of the more scenic stretches of the Oregon Coast. On a clear day, Mount Hood loomed on the northeast horizon.

The natural grandeur was lost on the men of the 70th, however, during the year they marched and bivouacked in its midst. Too many nights spent in pup tents and damp sleeping bags, too many days crawling through woods and underbrush soaked by the seemingly endless Oregon rain detracted from the splendor of their surroundings. Unfortunately, for many in the division, the poison oak that lurked in the lush foliage made life even more miserable. Les escaped the agony it caused, but as a medic he saw many who were not so lucky. "Since we slept in the woods so often, looking for a place to sleep that was clear of poison oak was paramount. Once the poison oak was on somebody's hands, other parts of the body were also affected—swollen eyes that made it impossible to see, and parts of the body that sent them to the hospital."

Physical conditioning was grueling. One final test required the men to do thirty-three push-ups and eleven sit-ups in twenty seconds before other rigorous timed trials. It ended with each man carrying a buddy of equal weight piggy-back for seventy-five yards and then cooling off by hiking four miles in fifty minutes.

Portland was considered a good leave town, but Les and his buddies didn't go there on weekends. "In those days, it was too far, with no freeway, and it cost too much. I didn't have any money. Half of my money went to Dad." Instead, they rode the army's big, olive-drab buses, or "cattle cars" as they called them, into Corvallis, nearby Albany, or the state capital, Salem, on off-duty weekends.

The Trailblazer trainees also had opportunity for relaxation and entertainment on post. Among other things, the division had its own dance band, three movie theaters, access to a good library, and a glee club that was a big favorite off post as well. The neighboring Oregonians were generous in their support of the troops. The USO sponsored dances and arranged for GIs to have dinner at civilian homes. But there was no substitute for going home on leave.

Les arrived at Camp Adair in August 1943. His first furlough home came in the latter part of April 1944. Traveling by train, his ten days away from camp went by quickly. "It took at least six days to travel—three one way, and three back, so I only had about four days at home."

His mother, shaken by her fifth son's conscription, had come to accept that he was in the army and would be going back to basic training; but she made sure that while he was home he had all his favorite things to eat. Life in Berne had not changed during his time away. Only one or two high school friends were still around. "A couple of guys, I think 4-F, were still in town. We went to a movie, or something; that's about it."

They also returned to the Palmer House, a prime example of small-town cafes where kids would hang out after school. Les said the owner knew them all. "He had a system where we could charge. We'd come in with a date, have a cherry Coke or a hamburger for fifteen cents or so and he'd let you charge." But he also had a limit that placed responsibility on the kids. "If your bill got up to, say, a dollar and a half, you had to pay it off before you could charge again."

Those four days at home passed all too quickly. When the Great Northern Railroad deposited him back in Oregon, he returned to the routine of digging foxholes, and sleeping on the ground. Throughout his time at Camp Adair, no mention was made of the 70th Division's combat destination. From their location on the West

Coast they more or less assumed they would go to the Pacific to fight the Japanese. Most of the motivational propaganda films they saw dealt with Japanese atrocities in China; few if any centered on what the Germans had done in Europe. It came as a complete surprise, then, when they were reassigned to Fort Leonard Wood, Missouri, in late July 1944, rather than to a port of embarkation in Portland, Seattle, or San Francisco.

Chill and dampness had been the Trailblazers' major complaint at Camp Adair, but now they were exchanging the cool Oregon summer for Missouri in July. As Les said, "Oregon was pretty nice, weather-wise, but now we're out digging foxholes in the clay, with thunderstorms overhead—I mean, hot and humid." Their training at Leonard Wood lasted through November.

At least they were in the Midwest, and close enough to Indiana that Les could contemplate another visit to the family. By November, however, all passes were frozen, and the men could not leave the post. A week or two before they were to ship out, Les and a buddy from Arkansas hatched a scheme to get home before they were sent overseas. They stole blank passes from the company orderly room, filled them out, and each signed the other's. Les hitchhiked to St. Louis and caught a train to Muncie, Indiana. Once on the train, he found that the MPs were, of course, checking passes. He avoided eye contact when he handed his pass to the MP. It turned out to be a memorable encounter.

"I'm sitting there thinking, 'Aw Jesus, if I get caught, oh no. . . .' So, I handed in my pass, and he stood there for a long time looking at the pass—didn't say anything. Pretty soon, he called his sergeant, and the sergeant looked at the pass, and said, 'Soldier, this is not a valid pass.' I tried to act dumb. I said, 'What do you mean, it's not valid?' 'Well,' he said, 'you can tell it's not a valid pass by the way it's signed.' I said, 'I got it from the captain, got the pass, and the—' He let me bury myself for a while, and pretty soon he said, 'Look, you know and I know that this is not a valid pass. I don't know why, but I'm going to let you go. But if you're not back at Leonard Wood on Monday morning for reveille, your ass is grass.'"

When the train reached Muncie, he thumbed his way the additional forty miles to Berne. On that early pitch-black Sunday morning in November, few vehicles came by; but he finally made it home for a brief visit. "I had no more than two hours, and they had to get me back." His brother Eli drove him to the train, and he made it back in time for reveille.

TASK FORCE HERREN

In the weeks following the June 6, 1944 D-Day landings in Normandy, U.S. Army casualties had for the most part been replaced with "fillers"—men picked straight from basic training and sent individually to units in Europe as needed. As casualties mounted and the need for infantrymen grew, three divisions were readied, their infantry regiments streamlined into task forces for quick deployment. Regiments of the 70th Division, including the 274th and its medical detachment, went under the command of General Thomas Herren, and bore the name Task Force Herren.

Components of the 70th Division departed Fort Leonard Wood on November 20, with their equipment stamped, "Port of Embarkation: Boston, Massachusetts." During his devious trip home shortly before the Trailblazers left, Les had told his father, "Don't tell Mom, but we're going overseas." On the three-day trip to Boston he tried to let his parents know that his journey had started. But letters written by combat-bound soldiers were being censored, and Les's report to his parents, "I went through Fort Wayne," fell to the censor's blackout pen.

The Trailblazers spent two weeks at Camp Miles Standish, just south of Boston, where they received newer equipment and had constant inspections. They received a short pass or two. Les spent his in Providence, Rhode Island, which was closer than Boston to the camp. Men in the 274th remembered that during those days of preparation they also "endured lectures on censorship, abandon-ship demonstrations, and sales talks on GI insurance and War Bonds." The time of anticipation finally ended, and the Trailblazers boarded ship for Europe on November 30, 1944.

A troop train took them to Boston in a pouring rain. It rolled right onto the dock, where a band was playing and Red Cross volunteers distributed donuts and coffee, and deposited the Trailblazers near the SS *Mariposa*, a converted luxury liner that the Matson Line had operated between San Francisco and Honolulu before the war. Les said they thought themselves fortunate going over, "in that we caught a former luxury passenger ship," but the heavily loaded men who trudged up the *Mariposa*'s gangplank with full gear were not embarking on a luxury cruise with an aloha welcome at the end of the voyage.

As Les's unit headed for the ship, someone was passing out little New Testaments. The men took them, and in the time-honored fashion of soldiers in every modern war, "we all stuck it over our hearts for protection." Then they clambered onto the gangplank, straight up into the ship. Once on board, they were directed "down, down, down, down to the very lowest of several decks." Their billet was a ten-man compartment deep in the bowels of the ship.

A monumental storm in the North Atlantic kept the *Mariposa* tied up at the dock for another day, and even though the weather would abate enough for their departure, more than one Trailblazer, including Les, had his first round of seasickness before they'd even left port.

Once under way, the first thing they learned was the importance of their life preservers. Les said, "I don't think I ever did anything without the life jacket. I slept in it, I walked in it." He laughingly recalled their "first warning."

"We all heard this sound that went 'ooogah, oooogah' and we thought, 'Oh my God, we've been hit. Already we've been hit.' So, we all jumped out of the hammocks, and we started running out. The navy guys running the ship, or the merchant marine—or whoever they were—were down there laughing at us. They had heard the claxton horn call for general quarters drill and routine control of the hold's watertight doors. But we all thought it was a sign we'd been hit."

By December 1944, the deadly threat of the German submarine wolf-packs had diminished somewhat, but more than enough U-boats remained active in the shipping lanes of the North Atlantic to be a constant danger. As one history of the 70th Division puts it, "Enough were freebooting farther south to make the voyage to the Straits of Gibraltar no pleasure cruise; troop ships were being sunk, . . . some with grave loss of life." Maintaining a strict blackout discipline, the three ships sailed alone rather than in convoy, and kept to a zig-zag course to avoid possible U-boat detection.

JOINING THE WAR

By the time the *Mariposa* had passed the Azores and reached Gibraltar, ocean traffic had picked up. Many on board, including Les, had never even seen the ocean before their army inductions; they all welcomed their first sight of land in nine days. "Passing through the Straits of Gibraltar was quite a sight," Les recalled. "Staring at the Rock, which I had read about in high school, was amazing. We could see Algiers on one side, and Spain on the other as we came through the entrance into the Mediterranean."

A Royal Navy cutter guided the *Mariposa* through the minefields off Gibraltar, and they kept to the south shore of the Mediterranean along the coast of Africa for two days. Les and his buddies wondered if German subs lurking below the surface were going to sink their ship—"and all of that made us anxious to debark." Finally, the *Mariposa* turned due north and entered the port of Marseille. The city was still dark, and the lights were on only on the docks. When the ship docked, the soldiers tossed pennies down on French workers below. One of the men aboard the *Mariposa* said, "I realized I was in a foreign land when I saw French workers on the Marseille docks wearing those little black berets."

They left the *Mariposa* on steel ladders down the side of the ship, onto the dock, and into the reality of the European Theater of Operations. Rubble was everywhere, sunken ships littered the harbor, dock warehouses stood gutted. The city had been shattered by heavy Allied bombing and left in near ruin by the Germans in retreat. A trip or two into the city while the 70th encamped nearby was enough to make Les think, *If I ever get back to Europe after the war, Marseille will not be a place I will visit.*

Trucked to their bivouac above the city, known as CP-2, the Trailblazers had a brutal introduction to conditions in Europe's worst winter in fifty years. A history of the division describes CP-2 as a "bleak plateau above the battered city. . . . There was not a single building in sight, trench and slit latrines were the only 'facilities.'" For the men of the 274th who arrived in France on December 10, it was back to pup tents and sleeping bags in the rain and mud. At night, the mud froze and snow fell, making conditions at Camp Adair idyllic in retrospect.

The more resourceful soldiers did business with their French neighbors, who sold them supplies of *vin ordinaire*. Though far from the finest Bordeaux, the common table wine contained enough alcohol to lessen their misery for a while. As the division history reports, "Wise officers developed myopia on inspection trips, and there was at least a modicum of pre-Christmas cheer in the vast encampment."

There would be precious little cheer from then on. The

Trailblazers were not afforded the customary time after landing on the Continent to become acclimated and receive additional training before entering combat. On December 16, the Germans launched a surprise attack on American forces in the Belgian Ardennes. What later became known as the Battle of the Bulge was on, and the 70th Division was soon dispatched northward. As Les recalled, "They got the message, 'Germans have broken through. Let's go.' So they hauled everybody onto trucks, and we moved out."

The 274th left CP-2 on December 20, 1944. They were destined to see action in the Vosges Mountains of Alsace, the province that had provided welcome refuge for Les Habegger's Swiss Anabaptist forebears three centuries earlier.

CHAPTER FOUR

A SEASON IN HELL

When orders came for the men of the 274th to depart Marseille on December 20, they did not regret leaving CP-2 and the icy blasts of the mistral wind that blows down the Rhone Valley. Les and his buddies had trained long and hard for what lay ahead, but nothing could have prepared them totally for some of the bloodiest action of World War II in the coldest winter Europe had seen in half a century.

The Battle of the Bulge began on December 16, 1944, when the Germans launched a surprise attack in the Belgian Ardennes, in an attempt to halt the Allied drive east and retake the port of Antwerp. Second only to the D-Day landings in Normandy, it may be the best-known combat sequence of World War II in Europe. But few know of a secondary Battle of the Bulge, fought south of the Ardennes in the French province of Alsace. It lasted longer and cost some 16,000 American casualties. It can be argued that the battle in Alsace was of greater significance than the more famous conflict in Belgium, because of its psychological, military, and political importance.

France and Germany had fought over the Alsatian lowlands along the Rhine and the wooded territory above the river for a century, and the Allies had just driven the occupying Germans out of Strasbourg in November 1944. Strasbourg held special significance for both nations, and retaking it would be a monumental propaganda stroke for the Germans. Militarily, if the Germans were to succeed in Alsace against the U.S. Seventh Army, it could stem the American counteroffensive in the Ardennes "Bulge." Politically, the loss of Alsace could well topple the fledgling government of General Charles de Gaulle in Paris.

Allied military intelligence knew in advance of Operation Northwind, as the Germans labeled their planned assault in Alsace. German forces north of the Saar River were to attack the Americans to the south, regain the area on the plain northwest of Strasbourg, divide the Seventh Army and link up with German forces in the "Colmar Pocket" along the Rhine.

The American Third Army, under General George Patton, went north to strengthen the beleaguered forces around Bastogne, and reserve components, only recently arrived in Europe, moved into the front lines in Alsace. Those untested units included the 70th Division's 274th Regiment and its medical detachment. Les Habegger received his battle star for the Ardennes-Alsace campaign.

MOVING FORWARD

In November 1944, the German 19th Army had crossed onto the western bank of the Rhine and were dug in south of Strasbourg around the city of Colmar. French forces were assigned to contain them in what became known as the "Colmar Pocket." The U.S. Seventh Army now stretched from points along the Rhine north and south of Strasbourg to a few miles beyond Saarbrucken on the Saar River to the northwest. The Seventh Army was responsible for keeping the Germans from reentering the Vosges Mountains, west of Strasbourg and south of Saarbrucken. General Eisenhower, the Allied Supreme Commander, ordered the Seventh Army, if attacked, to give ground slowly in the north as far back as the Vosges, but that a line must be held there.

Task Force Herren, now attached to the Seventh Army, headed north from Marseille on December 20. When the Trailblazers packed up to leave CP-2, on that flat and rocky hilltop above the city, the strategic importance and political significance of their movement could hardly have been further from their minds. Most men of the 274th made the four-day trip by rail, in small French freight cars known as "forty-and-eights" because their capacity was "forty men or eight horses." They had a cold and jolting ride, and arrived at Brumath, near Strasbourg, on Christmas Eve. Chaplains conducted religious services, and most men attended, having seen growing evidence of combat along the way. They felt a new and profound need for comfort and reassurance from their faith.

A dispatch unit of the 274th motored north, but it was no pleasure drive. Les and a fellow medic were selected to drive one of the battalion's forty or so jeeps loaded with gear and medical equipment. They had a bitterly cold and uncomfortable trip. The jeep's hand-operated windshield wiper was no match for the freezing rain that hit them head on. The dysentery that plagued many Trailblazers through that winter added to the misery. They reached Bischweiler, the regiment's intended destination, on Christmas Day. On the twenty-sixth, the 274th medics moved into the village of Herrlisheim on the Rhine.

German troops in massive concrete pillboxes across the river were in clear view of the Americans at Herrlisheim. "We got up in the morning and waved at each other," Les recalled from the few days the medics stayed there. "I can still see them over there. Nothing was happening in that sector at that time, but as we moved up, it was a different ballgame."

As Colonel Wallace Cheves, the regimental commander, later wrote, "There was very little danger in our positions at this time, but we were so green we didn't know it. . . . Occasional Kraut soldiers strolling carelessly among the pillboxes certainly didn't look like they were making war on anyone." Cheves also recalled that "beer and schnapps flowed freely at the local bars," and the men "felt like taking things easy and relaxing," but the warning of enemy patrols infiltrating behind their lines kept them on edge.

Their sector may have been quiet, but it was rife with rumors. Field orders from Task Force Herren's headquarters contained reports that enemy patrols from positions on the east bank were crossing the river onto the west side, under cover of darkness. "[They] rendezvous in groups of 200 or more for harassing and attack missions. . . . Enemy soldiers in U.S. uniforms, using U.S. equipment and vehicles, and enemy soldiers dressed as civilians may be encountered in the Task Force area." It was here that the regiment first experienced strafing by low-flying German aircraft, and they soon learned to take cover whenever the Luftwaffe appeared overhead. Here, too, the regiment sustained its first casualties when two men stepped on a land mine and were seriously wounded.

The 274th received its first combat assignment on December 27. They were to move out from Bischweiler and Herrlisheim and relieve elements of other infantry divisions along the Rhine. Its overall mission was to defend south of the Saar River near the French town of Bitche, which the Germans would soon hold. Trailblazers of another regiment, the 275th, were already in combat farther north and west. The terrain in which they fought was mountainous, heavily wooded, and punctuated by narrow valleys that ran north-south. Bitter cold and deep snow marked a pullback of American forces, including the 275th, to the town of Philippsbourg, where Les and his fellow medics saw their first action.

INTO THE BATTLE WITHOUT A GUN

On New Year's Eve, a report came that German paratroopers were landing in the vicinity west of Herrlisheim. Operation Northwind had begun in earnest. The next day, the 274th Medical Detachment left Herrlisheim, crossed through the Haguenau Forest, and reached the village of Niederbronn. They spent the night there in a large abandoned wire factory. Each rifle company had three medics, and as a medic in the first battalion, Les alternated between serving as a litter bearer and a company aid man. On the morning of January 4, First Battalion moved out toward Philippsbourg.

Les recalled that before they left Niederbronn, Captain Frank Ellis, the battalion surgeon, called the medics together inside the factory. "He said, 'Good luck. Just remember, the Germans shoot at medics.' That's what he said. I'll never forget that. Some Germans honored the Geneva Conventions, and some didn't. I'm sure some of our guys honored it and some didn't. My best buddy from Ohio got killed—a sniper got him. Shot him right in the middle of the red cross on his helmet." And so, with Captain Ellis's grim warning in mind, they struck off on the road to Philippsbourg.

The rifle companies had received their first ammunition in Bischweiler, and they realized then that this was the real thing. "Those troops marched out," Les said, "and we were behind them with the litters, marching down the road. And that's when we actually encountered the Germans, right there."

Basic training in the foothills around Camp Adair had simulated combat, but as Les often wondered, "How do you duplicate reality? In anything, we practice, practice, practice; but on that first day of combat, we were walking along with the rifle companies, and after a while we heard shells—artillery. Okay, we'd had that in training, big deal. I remember thinking, *Now, this is not too bad.* And the closer you got to the objective, the louder the noise became; and the more shells came; and pretty soon one hit in the road and everybody dove in the ditch. And now I'm saying, 'Wait a minute! This is different.' I kept thinking, *We trained for over a year, but you could train for ten years—it's not reality until you get to reality."*

He got to reality on the road to Philippsbourg and had to come to grips with its violence. "Wow, this isn't training any more. This is the real McCoy." He remembered seeing the first dead German and thinking, *Oh, Criminey! This is war. This is for real.* Fear, his companion in childhood, clutched at him again and did not loosen its hold until the war ended.

The small town of Philippsbourg stood as an important juncture on the road through the valley between Bitche and Niederbronn. Holding the town was crucial to containing the Germans in the Low Vosges and blocking them from any further advance south. The Trailblazers of the 275th who were already fighting at Philippsbourg had held positions there against a heavy German attack; but by January 4, they were in desperate need of help. First Battalion of the 274th was to attack and capture the hills west and northeast of town to lessen the pressure on the 275th. German troops held those hills on either side of town, and it fell to C Company, whose medics included Les Habegger, to take the hill on the west.

On the trek to Philippsbourg Captain Ellis and his aid-station technicians who were trained in suturing and giving plasma went by jeep, while Les and the other medics walked the five kilometers from Niederbronn with the rifle company. They made their way through a countryside shredded by artillery and reverberating with dreaded 88mm artillery blasts. The forested hills wore a blanket of fresh snow. The cold penetrated to a man's very core.

As Les recounted, "We're coming from the south, going north on this road, and just seventy-five to a hundred yards from town is where the captain set up the first aid station—right outside of town within artillery shell range. Our rifle companies were engaging the Germans in these hills, and that's where the casualties came from."

The civilians had mostly vacated the town. For their aid station, Captain Ellis took over a house, right where the fighting was going on. On the main road into town, it was not more than two hundred yards south of an intersection known as "88 Corner," so named because it took a relentless pounding from German 88mm artillery fire.

Les said, "The aid stations were always right next to the front lines, so I found myself right in the thick of the worst of it most of the time. Guys got hit, and if you were a litter bearer, you ran out with litters to get these guys and bring them in." In addition to bringing in casualties, his job included doing on-the-spot emergency first aid, which included stopping bleeding, applying tourniquets, giving morphine, and applying bandages. Once the wounded arrived at the aid station, Captain Ellis and his technicians took over. They immediately did what they could for a wounded man—getting plasma started into mangled bodies, clamping bleeding arteries in torn limbs—and then hustled him into an ambulance for transport back to the field hospital.

Throughout the medical corps, from litter bearer to combat surgeon, they dealt with a variety of wounds from small arms fire and shrapnel. A rifle wound was usually fairly clean, but shrapnel could be devastating. The shrapnel from artillery shells could leave wounds in a soldier's back, legs, stomach, head, and arms. It tore open flesh and broke bones.

The mountainous terrain at Philippsbourg compounded the difficulty for the litter bearers, sometimes making it difficult to keep from dropping the wounded. Exploding artillery shells meant having to drop the litter at times and hit the ground. Nature, too, exacted a toll. The brutal cold meant frostbite. Les said, "Frozen feet were a high-casualty item." He considered himself fortunate to have avoided that agony. "I was lucky, you know. You take your shoes off, and your socks off, and try to keep your feet moving—to get some circulation in there." But he had never been so cold. "In sub-zero conditions, we were sitting in foxholes, covered with snow, and it was—it was incredible."

From their original aid station, the men drove into Philippsbourg in a three-quarter ton truck to retrieve the wounded. The truck had a canvas cover over the bed with large Red Cross markings. Les recalled making one such retrieval on virtually the first day he was there. He and his companion in the truck bed that day had been in the same barracks at Camp Adair. Milton had kept Les and everyone else awake with his nocturnal babbling and ranting. "You could hear him talking, and he was swearing—cussing the Germans, cussing Roosevelt, and cussing Hitler, and he'd say, 'You wait 'til we get over there. I'll show those blankety-blank-blanks—I'll get those guys.'"

On this particular day, they drove into Philippsbourg, and as they neared 88 Corner, Les recalled, "Milton and I were in the back of the truck going in to get the wounded. As the truck neared the intersection—bingo!—in comes the artillery. The driver of the truck put on the brakes, and Milton and I dove out of the back end of the truck into the ditch. The last time I saw Milton, he was running down the ditch, running as fast as he could—he absolutely cracked. And that was the end of his combat. They sent him home."

Sometimes, Les thought he was just about as scared as Milton must have been, and he would ask himself, "How did I get through all of it? Why didn't I just get up and run away too; or, better yet, get myself wounded on purpose just so I could get out of there? Believe me, I wasn't the only one who thought about those things on occasion. But those thoughts notwithstanding, we just kept going at it day in and day out and somehow I survived. I guess that's what it means to face your fears. You don't always overcome them, but you can beat them."

They worked out of the same aid station for a while until the captain moved them into Philippsbourg proper. Dr. Frank Ellis, not long out of medical school, had come to the 274th Medical Detachment at Fort Leonard Wood just before its departure. Les said, "He was tough, meaning he expected everyone to do everything possible to treat the wounded and get them to a field hospital as fast as possible. As a young kid, I looked up to him and respected him very much."

They set up the second aid station just beyond 88 Corner, in a typical Alsatian house with living quarters above the barn. Les described the setting: "We had our aid station upstairs. Shelling hit the roof, and I can still remember the shells landing all around us while we were treating the wounded there. As a matter of fact, in the basement of this aid station was Company D's command post—they had their headquarters down there. The Germans threw a delayed shell that went through the roof and exploded in the basement and killed I don't know how many guys down there—smattered them all over the place in the basement of our aid station."

One of the survivors of that blast was Sergeant Charlie Schlagel from Texas, who had been in charge of First Battalion's basic training at Camp Adair. Few soldiers ever forgot their drill sergeants, and Les had good reason to remember his. "Oh yeah, Schlagel. He was the sergeant. He was a good guy, but he was a tough guy—a true drill sergeant. And I'll never forget, in training he would walk up and down the barracks in the morning and he'd say, 'You better give your heart to Jesus, because your ass is mine.' Every day, he would say that. He was a tough guy, an older guy. Well, Charlie was in the basement when that shell went through, but he came out of it alive. And after that, whenever the chaplain got up there to hold services, Charlie was in the front row."

CLOSE CALLS AND MIRACLES

Les had his own share of close calls and miracles. Company C had wounded men lying in the snow up in the hills west of town. They had been there for a few days, but could not be reached because the Germans had them surrounded. Calls kept coming in to "get these wounded out of there." Les would never forget what happened next.

As they had learned at Herrlisheim, some Germans had infiltrated the American lines, capturing equipment and uniforms. At Philippsbourg, intelligence sources reported English-speaking Germans wearing American uniforms. U.S. troops wore heavy steel helmets and helmet liners over brown woolen skullcaps. The Trailblazers were told that the infiltrating Germans were not wearing American helmets, but they had the woolen caps on. The men had this clearly in mind when Captain Ellis said, "We've got to go up and get these guys."

Les was one of six men sent to bring in the wounded, accompanied by a rifle squad in case they encountered Germans. They left the aid station and started up a forty-five degree slope at 2:30 or 3:00 in the morning. In the pitch black and bitter cold, fighting neck-deep snow, they climbed and reached the men without encountering any Germans. They placed the severely wounded on the litters. One rifleman had shrapnel wounds in his head and shoulder, but as Les recalled, "He could walk, so we made him walk, and put the others on the stretcher. I was the guy who helped him walk—I helped him get back to the aid station."

With his arm around the soldier's waist and the man leaning on him, Les supported him back down the hill, as if helping a player with a sprained ankle off the basketball court. Les described their return: "We were a lot slower than the guys with the litters, but we got through, and back into town. When we finally hit the streets of Philippsbourg, the fellows with the litters—and the rifle squad that had gone with us—took off real fast on the streets." They left Les, still supporting the wounded man, shuffling toward the aid station.

"All of a sudden, I saw a guy jump out from behind a building, and he stuck a pistol in my side and said, 'Where are you from?'"

As the figure had run at him, Les saw he was wearing an American uniform and a skullcap, but no helmet. "If he was an American, he was crazy. There was no reason for an American to do this to me, another American."

The next minute or so seemed an eternity.

"My mind and heart were racing a mile a minute. *What should I do?* There was no doubt in my mind that he was a Kraut. Even if it was a GI who had gone nuts, what could I do? Helping an injured soldier walk and carrying only medical supplies, I was hardly a match for a man with a pistol in my side. It's interesting what goes through your mind at such a moment. *What do I do? What do I say?*"

The German kept saying, "Where are you from? Where are you from?"

Les replied, "What do you mean? You know where."

"What state are you from?"

Les decided the man wanted information that he could use to get more information—so he could say to somebody, for example, "I'm from Missouri," and impersonate an American. Les picked a state at random.

"He kept walking along with me for a while, and asked, 'What town are you from? Where have you been holed up?'" Les said he thought of naming a town in a different state, "But then, jeez, what if he knows American geography well enough to know that city isn't in that state?"

They continued on for a few more steps, "which seemed like miles," before the German vanished behind a building as fast as he had appeared.

One English-speaking German soldier captured during the Ardennes-Alsace action had asked his captors the same sorts of questions Les heard that day. He claimed to have been in training for work in administration abroad that would follow Hitler's ultimate conquest of North America. Les's pistol-wielding German might well have belonged to that elite group, who spoke accent-free English.

When he reached the aid station, Les reported the incident to Captain Ellis. The rifle squad sent to search found no trace of the German. Decades later, Les continued to ask himself, "Why didn't he take me prisoner? There were probably several reasons why, but not pulling the trigger is another thing. I guess it was my lucky day."

At no small cost, the men of the 274th had succeeded in taking and holding the town of Philippsbourg. Colonel Cheves proudly wrote, "[They] had accomplished the task of stemming the rapid advance of furious SS Mountain troops in their wild drive to the Alsatian Plain. Despite the hardships and grueling hours of fighting in the snow, . . . [they had held] their ground to the very inch when the regiment received orders to withdraw."

Those SS troops, under the personal command of Heinrich Himmler, had already forged south on both the east and west around Philippsbourg. They now launched a drive into Philippsbourg itself.

The 274th Medical Detachment spent two frigid weeks at the Philippsbourg aid stations. On January 16, 1945, word came to pull back. As Les Habegger remembered, "The word came that we had to get out. The Germans had pushed through, and we had to run and get out of there—or we would get captured. Some of our guys—not medics, but a lot of our rifle companies—got captured there. A whole bunch of them. Literally whole companies were captured. We had to run for our lives. I remember jumping on the jeep, and they told us, 'Don't take anything! Leave it, and let's go!' So, we took off down the road, and eventually ended up—I can't recall where, but we drove, and drove, and drove 'til we reached someplace safe, and we spent the night in a barn. I remember crawling into the hay in the barn, and we slept there that night; and I still remember the feeling when we hit that hay of being so thankful."

He thanked the Lord. "'God, I'm in a barn. I'm not in a foxhole. I'm dry. I'm warm. I'm in hay.' I was thankful, because we had gotten out of there."

Foxhole Fears

During the entire Philippsbourg ordeal, Les lived in fear every day. He asked himself, "Am I going to die, or am I not going to die?" He later saw that, given his upbringing and the impact of his grandfather's hellfire preaching, such introspection was, for him, extremely powerful. "I had heard about all this hell stuff to the point that one time I went to see a chaplain."

The young Amish man was not expecting a Roman Catholic chaplain, but in near desperation he unburdened himself anyway. He told the priest, "I've gotta have some help, because I'm scared to death and I don't know how to respond—how to handle this fear."

"Well, we're all scared," the chaplain replied.

"Yeah, but you don't understand. If I get killed, I'm going to hell."

When the chaplain asked if he ever prayed, Les said, "Do I ever pray? I never stop praying!"

"Do you have a rosary?"

"No, sir, I'm not a Catholic. I'm a Protestant."

"Well, it doesn't make any difference," the chaplain said. "We have stories of people who had rosaries whose lives were spared. Here, take this rosary."

When Les asked for instructions, the chaplain said, "Take it, and when you pray it, count the beads on there as you pray."

"What does that do?" Les asked.

"Just do it!"

He still had the New Testament in his breast pocket and thought, *Well, okay. I've got the heart covered. Maybe this rosary might do something. Like a rabbit's foot.* He took the beads and put them in his pocket, but he felt guilty. He carried the rosary for a long time before the source of his guilty feelings finally came to him. "If I get killed, they will send my belongings home to Mom; and if she finds a rosary, it'll kill her. I can't do that. I can't do that to my mother." He decided to take his chances without it, and threw the rosary off into the trees.

Throughout January, the 70th Infantry Division had been stymied—holding on here, making small gains there, pulling back. By mid-February, events turned more to the Americans' favor. They would soon move north, cross the Saar River, take the city of Saarbrucken, and drive further into Germany. But winter kept its merciless hold on the Low Vosges as the 274th moved northwest in the direction of Sarreguemines, France. Victories were hard won.

Les spent the next six to eight weeks in foxholes. "We were on the front, never relieved for eighty days. It seemed I never got out of that foxhole. I remember getting a shower once in that whole time. We of course lived in our clothes. In a foxhole, you can't get out of there. We did the best we could, and we had rations. But I don't remember us getting a hot meal in . . . I can't tell you how many days." They lived on C-rations, which came in cans, and K-rations that were in boxes "like Cracker Jack boxes."

Early in the drive north, when Les got out of the foxhole on one occasion, he put part of a K-ration to good use, devising a special treat for himself.

"The K-ration included a bar about the size of a Milky Way, a chocolate bar, but it was hard as a rock. It was meant to give you some energy if you could chew it, but it was just hard as a rock. I remember one time, we had a butane burner and I took that chocolate bar, and I melted it—put it in my mess kit, put it on the burner, and melted it—and then went out and got snow. There was a farmer—I don't know where—and I went over with my melted chocolate and snow, and asked him for some milk. I got me a chocolate milkshake with that."

Culinary delights were few and far between. On the subject of food, Les recalled, "I remember sitting in a foxhole, and the guys would talk. We didn't have any food, we were hungry. I wouldn't think of a steak or something, I'd think of Mom's pies or apple dumplings—I loved apple dumplings, and stuff like that. As a matter of fact, she sent me a pecan pie to the front lines. I got it six weeks after she shipped it, and it was like it just came out of the oven—*oh!*" She had sent a whole pie, wrapped in cellophane and packed in real popcorn to keep it moist. Les laughed when asked if he had to share it. "Well yeah, or get shot."

RUBBLE, RUINS, AND THE RHINE

By the end of February, the snow had melted and Trailblazers of the 274th had driven the stubborn enemy back out of the Low Vosges. They had taken Kreutzberg Ridge, Forbacherberg Ridge, Etzlingen, Spicheren—and finally Spicheren Heights, which looked down over a wide plain and the town of Stiring-Wendel. The plain lay between the Trailblazers and their ultimate goal: Saarbrucken, on the German side of the Saar River.

Several times since January 4, on the road to Philippsbourg, shells had landed near Les, knocking off his helmet, and showering him with rocks and dirt, but no shrapnel. "Those were instances where you think you're going to die—and by the grace of God—but you say, 'Well, okay, I survived.'"

When the 274th reached Spicheren Heights on the drive to the Saar, they set up an aid station in the village of Etzlingen. There, Les lived through another close call and miraculously escaped unharmed.

Once the area had been secured, he and four riflemen stood around talking while one of them started digging a foxhole. The hole had barely reached a depth for one man when they heard the unmistakable sound of an incoming 88. All five men dove for the hole. Les, the farthest away, landed on top of the other four—well above ground and totally exposed. The shell landed close by and again he was covered with dirt and rocks but no shrapnel. The only man in the group to be hit was the first rifleman into the hole, the man who had done the digging. Lying on the bottom, covered by the other four, he was somehow wounded—and severely enough to be evacuated back home. Les has asked himself many times since, "How did I survive that? Being a believer in God and a Christian, I choose to believe that only by the grace of God can it be explained."

German artillery pounded the Trailblazers with intensity on the ridge above the Saar plain. With Saarbrucken as their goal, early on March 3 they moved down on the town of Stiring-Wendel on the French side of the river. It was defended by formidable pillboxes and the entire sector was heavily mined. The snow had turned to rain, and the foxholes filled with mud, further battering the 247th with the miseries of war.

According to Colonel Cheves, "The drive on Saarbrucken was a nightmare from the beginning." Their advance was painfully slow, but by late March, the regiment had moved into the city. Les and the medics crossed the Saar by jeep on a pontoon bridge built by army engineers. Even after all he had seen since Marseille, he was stunned by the destruction.

"The city was gone. All I can remember is enough room between the rubble for one jeep. Some of the civilians had thrown flowers on top of the rubble, signifying that there were people dead underneath the rubble. It was absolutely destroyed to the ground. Just shelling, shelling, shelling—and the bombing . . ."

They left the ruins of Saarbrucken behind and pushed on into Germany. In the Ardennes, in the Belgian Battle of the Bulge, the German offensive had failed. Their armies pulled back all along the line, and the Allies crossed the Rhine from Bingen on to the north. Les recalled, "It didn't take us very long from Saarbrucken to get to the Rhine, because the Germans were running the whole way."

By April 15, they had reached the Rhine, which was where they were when they heard the news of President Roosevelt's death. Few Trailblazers had memory of any president other than FDR. Les recalled, "We were all saying, 'Who's the vice president?' Nobody knew who the guy was."

On their way to the Rhine, they had met only a smattering of fighting—skirmishes, but nothing to equal what they had seen in the Vosges, where these boy soldiers had grown quickly into men. The 274th Medical Detachment crossed the Rhine at Mainz on a recently built pontoon bridge. Troops of the 70th Infantry Division remained as an occupying force in such places as Bad Kreuznach, Kaiserslautern, Mainz, and Wiesbaden until October 1945, when a majority of them sailed for home. But Les was not among them.

A town the size of Berne, Indiana, kept track of its servicemen. Everyone in town knew when a telegram arrived to inform a family of a battle casualty. Les's brother Eli told him later that when news of a telegram hit town, "they'd wonder, *was it me?*"

Since boarding the *Mariposa* in Boston Harbor, Les had sent letters home infrequently, at best. And then he could only tell them he was "somewhere in France." From newspaper and radio accounts, his father had been able to track the whereabouts of the 70th Infantry Division, so they knew he was in the thick of the fighting. His sister Martha recalled how their mother worried about him.

"Mother had a hard time coping with Les's army duty. She had five boys in the service, but only Les was really in combat. Sometimes we didn't hear from him for a month. And after the war ended, it was three weeks before we knew whether he survived or not. It was really hard." She said she could never go to her parents' house and find them happy. "They were always concerned about Les."

Les had feared his grandfather's hell ever since childhood. It had vividly appeared to him in the hot coals and flames of the family stove in Indiana. True hell and true fear had found him in the ice, snow, and piercing, relentless cold of the Vosges Mountains; in the thunder of incoming shell fire and the roar of automatic weapons; in the hideously wounded casualties he treated and delivered to the 274th's aid stations. He had come through hell unscathed—but he wondered how and why—except by the grace of God—he had survived.

CHAPTER FIVE

POSTWAR ADVENTURES IN EUROPE

After the 70th Infantry Division crossed the Rhine, it became part of the Army of Occupation. The 274th Regiment and its medical detachment pushed on into Wiesbaden. There, Les's fluency in German became as useful to the army as his skill as a medic. Occasionally, his new duties challenged his Amish values.

When they reached Wiesbaden, the regiment commandeered civilian houses for billeting American troops. Les said, "I didn't leave Europe to come home until March of '46, and the whole time I was there, I lived in German houses." To put it bluntly, "They sent me around to get into houses and kick the Germans out, and we would move in. The unit commander would send a rifleman with me, and we'd knock on the door and say, 'This is the United States Army. We're taking over your house. You have forty-five minutes to get out—and this is what you can take. The rest of the stuff you leave.' And we'd let them take some bedding, and a few kitchen things, but everything else stayed. They would scream and holler—especially the women, and I thought of my mom every time. I never went up to a door without thinking, 'If Mom would see me now, she'd just absolutely—" By that time, however, he had reached the point of thinking that he was only balancing the scales.

"One thing war does, it hardens you. And I remember thinking, 'Okay, I didn't ask to come over here. I've been sleeping on the ground for months. It's your turn now.' That was kind of the attitude. And as cold as it sounds, it was really the truth. . . . We didn't destroy anything. It wasn't a matter of that sort of thing, but we were there."

Victory in Wiesbaden

When the war in Europe officially ended on May 8, 1945, the BBC broadcast the news out of London. Someone with a radio came running out of the house in Wiesbaden yelling, "The war is over! The war is over!" Les said that the 274th Regiment soon found "the best way to celebrate."

"Our billet was three or four blocks from a winery and champagne bottling works. I remembered that the son of a family living nearby had a little red wagon, and I confiscated the red wagon and went up to the champagne and wine place." The Germans in town, and at the winery, had no luxuries such as candy, coffee, cigarettes, soap, and the like. Les, who did not smoke then, took cigarettes and some coffee and bartered with them. "I got enough wine and champagne bottles to fill up the wagon. I took them back and we celebrated through the night—and more nights after."

During his time in Wiesbaden, he observed the destruction of the German infrastructure, which was "absolutely gone," just as it had been in Saarbrucken. He went to Frankfurt, and it was the same story. "It was gone, you know—*everything*. Just enough room for a jeep to drive through." When he got to Cologne, he found the cathedral still standing.

"You wonder sometimes—war is a terrible thing, but somehow certain things were spared. The old cathedral—it was a weird sight to see everything in rubble, and then here are these spires still standing. Otherwise, the devastation was indescribable."

In many of those places, the people were literally starving, as well. Les said, "They had no food. They had nothing." The house they commandeered for their billet stood next to the one taken for the regimental kitchen, where the GIs were fed very well.

"After the meals at the kitchen, they would pour the coffee grounds out on a drain there, and I can remember seeing kids—their mothers would send them out with big cans, and they'd scoop up the coffee grounds. They were hungry. And I remember giving candy bars and stuff to the little kids—at that time, they had nothing. And there was a German girl I met—I remember bringing food to her family because they didn't have any." Even if there had been food to buy, rampant inflation would have put it out of reach for most German families.

When the war ended, General Eisenhower imposed on his troops a policy of non-fraternization with civilians. As Les interpreted it, "You will not fraternize with the enemy. There will be no talking. You do not go into German homes—nothing. If you did, and they caught you, you got court-martialed. The problem was that men being men, and boys being boys, they were going to find the girls during the day, and visit them at night." Because of the non-fraternizing rule, "the guys would not come into our aid station for prophylactics. So we started having a lot of gonorrhea and venereal disease." Eisenhower soon realized the futility of his policy and rescinded it.

When the restrictions on visiting were lifted, Les met a young Fräulein in the city. "I had a little girlfriend in town there, sure." Putting his German to further use, he explored how World War II could have happened—how Hitler could have come to power. "I would go into German homes, and I was really interested about this war—how did all this happen? When I would meet people, Germans, I would start talking to them. They'd say, 'Come and have a glass of wine.' And I would go at night to their homes." He often thought that "any real Nazis could have done away with me." But he went and talked with them, and said, "Tell me how this happened. I want to know about this whole thing. Of course, I never met a person who said they were for Hitler. They all hated him—you know how that goes. But I would talk to these people, and I really enjoyed getting their perspective. Some would rationalize by comparing the United States and Germany, and they would say, 'We had Hitler, and you had Roosevelt. Both came in about the same time, and both our countries were in the Depression. We needed work. Your president built roads and other projects. Our president built tanks and guns.'"

Others added pragmatic considerations to their rationalizations. "They would say, 'But I'm a father. I have children. Am I going to ask questions when I have a job? And when we—when everybody looked around—when Hitler really got control, it was too late.' So you know they were rationalizing, but still I really enjoyed talking, and I talked to people a lot about the war."

Les had earlier seen an unsavory and tasteless postwar ploy used by some in dealing with their drastically altered situations. He laughed ruefully when he recalled his job of commandeering billets. "When the Germans got wind of what we were doing—that we were taking over homes—every once in a while you'd see a nice house that you wanted, and on the gate of the fence—they had these wrought iron fences—there would be a sign in German: "Wir sind Juden." You know, 'We are Jews.' Yeah—"

A New Kind of Drill

Once the European war ended, the men of the 70th Infantry Division assumed they would be sent to fight in the Pacific Theater. Some units had already begun training for amphibious landings. Then the first atomic bomb destroyed Hiroshima on August 6, 1945. No one knew what lay ahead, but as the history of the division puts it, "Trailblazers could only exult that they would not be cannon fodder on the beachheads of Japan."

Final, unconditional surrender, on August 25, made returning home uppermost in their minds. A priority point system had been worked out that assigned value to various factors. As Les put it, "Points determined when you'd get to come home, depending on how long you'd been in, how long you'd been overseas, and whether you had family at home—a wife, children." Men with a high number of points got to go home first. "Those of us who didn't got sent to another division."

In July 1945, Les was transferred to the 3rd Division. Its aid station was in the town of Hersfeld, northeast of Frankfurt. "It was a nice size city," Les recalled, "but I soon found myself in the small town of Tann, with a rifle company who were out on the line across from the Russians."

That little village, southeast of Hersfeld, lay just inside what became the clearly marked border between East and West Germany. "There was no fence in 1946, but the Russians were there and we were there—and we bartered with them, traded stuff. But everybody carried their guns."

Life in Tann, which Les called a "dinky town, way down there in the sticks," lacked any attraction for the young American soldiers. When one of Les's buddies at the aid station in Hersfeld asked if he wanted to go back up there, he jumped at the chance.

The aid station in Hersfeld functioned primarily as a first aid dispensary and a prophylactic station. The staff included one dentist, for both officers and enlisted men. Les transferred there in September, but he needed to serve in some way while he waited to go home, so he became the dentist's assistant. With no electricity, they relied on a foot-powered dental drill, and part of Les's duties included manning the foot pump and mixing the amalgam for fillings.

One of the more amusing incidents of Les's military career played out in the dentist's office. Each morning, he and the dentist checked the day's appointment sheet together. On one memorable day, the dentist told Les, "'At ten o'clock, we've got Major W—. I hate the S.O.B. Now, when he gets in the chair and I start drilling, I want you to pump *very slowly*.' I remember he's grinding—eerrrrrrrr—and I'm pumping nice and slow, because he hated this guy and he wanted him to suffer! True story." Les's stint as a dental assistant lasted until January 1946 when he was finally slated to return home.

Les also became a vital cog in the social life of the regimental surgeon. The army maintained a hospital in Kassel, about thirty miles from Hersfeld, with a staff of army nurses. "Kassel was up north," Les said, "and the major had a lady friend up there, so my job was to transport her down to Hersfeld on Friday nights, and then take her back to the hospital on Sunday." He did not elaborate on any conversations they may have had en route.

ALPINE ADVENTURES

Les's opportunity for travel extended beyond his sorties between Hersfeld and Kassel. He took advantage of an army furlough program that allowed soldiers to choose a travel destination but put a limit on the number allowed to visit each place. "If your first choice was full, you had to pick an alternate. Of course, I chose Switzerland, but I couldn't go to the area where my grandparents were born (Bern) because of the cap on how many could visit a specific region. There were probably four different tours within Switzerland. The only one available for me was the one that went to the Italian border." He made the trip from Hersfeld down to Basel in a five-ton Army truck, and from there by train to Zurich and Lucerne, and on to Lugano on the Italian border via the long tunnel through the Alps. He returned by the same route.

On the way down, he had some time in Basel before boarding the train.

"I was anxious to try my Swiss, to see if they spoke the same way that my folks taught us, so I went into a gift shop." He was sporting a pipe at the time, and it was raining, so he turned the pipe over to keep the tobacco dry. "When I walked into the gift shop, two sales clerks behind the counter looked at me, and one said, 'Look at that crazy American; he has his pipe turned upside down.' So I went over to them and said, 'I'm not as crazy as you think. I'm keeping my tobacco dry.' They both wanted to know if I was Swiss. We had a good conversation, and it was gratifying to know that we spoke the real Swiss in our home in Indiana."

He had a similar language experience on a street corner in Lucerne. He asked two young men near his age about distances from Lucerne.

"I went up to them and asked in Swiss how far it was to Bern. They answered me in English. I wanted to let them know that I spoke Swiss, and they wanted to show me that they could speak English. We spent quite a bit of time together, and on the way back I saw them again." They could not believe that the army granted leaves for visiting family members in Switzerland only to those going to see grandparents and immediate family. Later, Emil Koller, one of the two young Swiss men, wrote to the commanding officer in Hersfeld:

> My school fellow and I had met on the 26 October in Lucerne Mr. Habegger. . . . I had been astonished to hear that his grandparents had been expatriated from Bern to America and he speaks still well "Bern-deutsch." He told us that one of his cousins lives in Bern. . . . We don't [think] it fair that GIs of Swiss origin are not allowed to stay longer than eight days in Switzerland. Therefore

we beg to ask you for a further Switzerland leave for Mr. Habegger. Please, examining my request, consider that his last leave fell in a raining season. Hoping you might agree with us, we look forward to the visit of Mr. Habegger, who is always welcome by us.

Les said, "Naturally the request was denied. I was thankful and lucky to go anyplace."

Denied the opportunity to locate his cousins, Les did have the fun of seeing the family name on businesses in Zurich. He recalled that another GI in his tour group had brought it to his attention. "One of the guys said, 'Hey, I saw your name over here on a store!' So I went over, and here was Habegger Tobacco. So I walked in, and of course he didn't know—and I didn't know—where on the family tree we were, but there were a whole bunch of Habeggers around there in that area." He might well have bought his new pipe in that tobacco store.

HOOPS COME TO HERSFELD

Life was good. Looking back, Les said, "Those days were the best possible life I ever had. Because the war was over, there was no training." When the regiment formed a basketball team in Hersfeld, it was icing on the cake for Les.

While Les was a medic-in-training at Camp Adair, the Trailblazers had conducted a sports program, but his schedule had kept him from taking part. He described returning to the game after more than a year's absence: "I saw a sign that said anyone interested in trying out for the regiment's team should report to the gym. I went, and they already had players that had played some in college—one for the University of Minnesota, and one from Illinois. I shocked them and ended up as a starting guard. We played different units in Germany, but I don't remember how many games we played."

Perhaps Amish modesty prevented his giving a complete picture of things. Press accounts with headlines such as, "RHQ Five Triumphs Over Service Company Quintet As Lester Habegger Stars, 33-13," provided more detail. The team was "sparked by their effervescent forward, Lester Habegger, . . . [who] registered the initial counter of the game when he dropped in a two-handed pivot shot."

The Service Company team "kept plugging" until early in the second period, before "Habegger . . . took charge for the boys from Regiment. . . . The steady, if not gaudy, efforts of Habegger were a steady source of concern to the harassed Service five. . . . Habegger was the standout performer of the evening and led all scorers with sixteen points." Les gave the team his steady (and flashy) play from October through December, but basketball ended abruptly when he began the journey home in early January 1946.

"We left Hersfeld, bound for Stuttgart, to wait for a train that would take us someplace where we could get on a ship and come home. We waited for about a month, and we had no duty, so we just wandered around. We did spend a lot of time at the service club, drinking coffee and eating donuts."

Les also made a memorable visit to the Stuttgart Opera House, which had served as a club for French and American military just after the war.

The smaller of the Stuttgart State Opera houses had been destroyed by heavy Allied bombing. The other building survived the war, one of few opera houses in Germany to do so. Les said, "I read in the newspaper that the opera house was opening for the first time after the war and thought it would be a historic event to be a part of." When it reopened in February 1946, he and a couple of other soldiers from his unit were in the audience. They saw a performance of Paul Hindemith's classic *Matis der Maler*, sung in German for the first time after the war.

HOMEWARD BOUND

After devoting their February to culture, sightseeing, and coffee-drinking, in March Les and his buddies left Stuttgart on a train bound for the Belgian port of Antwerp. The troop ship waiting for them at the dock was a far cry from the SS *Mariposa* that had delivered them safely into Marseille some fourteen months earlier.

That small, converted cargo vessel, *Marine Raven*, provided the last of Les's terrifying wartime experiences.

"The voyage home was worse than the war. I thought I was going to die many times during the war—I had experiences that I haven't talked about—but that boat coming back . . . we were like a cigar box on that ocean. We set sail into the English Channel, and already we had a storm."

The Channel storm was only the beginning. Across the North Atlantic, they rode forty- to forty-five foot waves day after day, in the worst series of storms imaginable.

As luck would have it, Les said that when they finally boarded the *Marine Raven*, "I ended up in a bunk in the bow. That first night, I said, 'No, I'm not going to do this. I'm not going to be down here like this.' A couple of my buddies were in the back of the ship in the middle, so I went back and slept on the floor back there with them."

No spot below decks would have eased the discomfort. Waves washed over the ship constantly, and the crew wouldn't let the passengers up on deck because the water was coming over the rails. Foul air and inadequate latrines made life miserable. "Everyone was seasick—nobody was eating. And if you did, you lost it soon after you ate. Things were just . . . ugh." This continued for the entire twelve-day crossing. At times Les thought, *My God, we survived Hitler, but now we're all going to drown.*

Never had drowning seemed so imminent as when they reached the mouth of the Hudson River in New York. Les was convinced the ship would capsize when the thousand or so men on board all rushed to the port side for a reassuring glimpse of the Statue of Liberty. Calm prevailed, and with balance restored, they received a well-deserved hero's welcome. "They met the boat with dancing girls and a band, and welcome home—and, oh yeah, it was a big deal."

Late in the day, they moored at a pier upriver near the George Washington Bridge, where they had to spend one more night on board. When Les finally touched solid ground, he had one more military run-in.

"We got off the ship, and I ran to a pay phone that was right there on the dock. One of the MPs grabbed me and said, 'You can't make a phone call if you're going overseas.' I said, 'The hell I can't! I just got off that ship and called my mother.'"

Most of the troops were put on a ferry to Camp Kilmer, over in New Jersey. Les "got commandeered" to go with the supply truck. "So, I got to ride with a bunch of equipment on a truck" across the George Washington Bridge. From Camp Kilmer, Les was sent straight to Camp Attebury, outside of Indianapolis, where he stayed only long enough to receive his discharge.

He had served honorably and well, as his decorations and citations attested. Among them were the EAME (European-African-Middle Eastern) Campaign Medal, with three Bronze Stars for service in the Ardennes, Rhineland, and Central Europe. He also received the American Theater Ribbon, the Good Conduct Medal, the Combat Medical Badge, and the Army of Occupation Badge. Of considerable significance, his record contains a letter of unit commendation from the corps commander for action before and after the taking of Saarbrucken. It states: "The courage of your men is evident in their victory in the face of the enemy's stubborn resistance," to which the

70th Division's commanding general added, "All members of the team may be justly proud of the above recognition of the combat efforts of the Division."

The young man who returned to Indiana that spring might have looked like the boy who had climbed on a bus in Decatur, bound for the induction center nearly three years before, but he was not the same person. The war had brutally forced maturity on him. Les Habegger had seen and done things that were beyond his imagining in July 1943. He now saw the world differently; he felt that it had to hold bigger and better things for him.

CHAPTER SIX

CHAPTER SIX

BACK HOME IN INDIANA

Once the war ended, Americans demanded a swift return of their servicemen, and the Truman Administration speeded demobilization. By the time Les departed Stuttgart, the four other Habegger brothers had already returned safely home. Young men now trickled back one by one, and any sense of a need for civic celebration had worn off. Veterans began to recognize that the country had changed during the war, and they wondered where they fit into its future. Les felt that Berne had changed little, and his stoic and undemonstrative family not at all; but the war had changed him, and his future was uncertain.

His brother Dave had resumed working in Berne's furniture factory after his discharge from the army; he and his wife, Maxine, and their two daughters were living with her mother in Indianapolis. Maxine met Les at the train station and drove him home to Berne. They arrived just as school let out for the afternoon. As they drove up to the family home, the kids from the area were walking by, coming home from school. Les knew them. They had been freshmen when he left; now, their lives and his could not have been any more different.

Things had indeed changed since his graduation from Berne High School. All of his siblings were married and on their own, leaving Jacob and Rosina alone in the family home.

"When I got there, only Mom was home. Dad, and of course my brothers, were working, so it was just Mom. I don't remember getting a kiss; I don't know if I got a hug. I might have, but—"

Rosina soon erased some of his disappointment, when, as his sister Martha recalled, "Mom had us all home for a Sunday meal to welcome him home."

Control of their emotions was a hallmark of the Habegger family. Les said, "I don't remember seeing any demonstrations of love. We all knew, or assumed, we were loved, and we were, but Dad came from the old school, and emotions were not regarded."

Still, Les had hoped for a heartfelt welcome home from his father. "When we came home, the feeling was that you want to be greeted as a hero." But when Jacob came in from work that day, he made no special acknowledgement of Les. "It was kind of like 'Hi, nice to see you,' or something like that." It was business as usual, almost as if Les had just come from basketball practice after school.

WAR AND PEACE COLLIDE

In his years away, Les had wondered many times what his mother might have thought of his wartime activities, especially during the year of occupation in Germany. Having been thrust into the savage reality of war, he was now squarely *of* the world as well as in it.

He wondered whether anyone could understand what he had seen and what he had done since his high school graduation. Would his family still see him as the baby and expect him to obediently resume that role? He could remember sitting in a foxhole saying, "Wait a minute. I'm supposed to have been this little baby that's not going to—why the hell am I here, and they're back in the States?" His brothers, too, had served, but only Les had seen true combat.

Now he wondered, "How can I sit down and say, 'Okay, here's what happened?'" Even if he could have found words to describe the horror and terror he had lived with, he doubted that any of his family would have wanted to know. "They wouldn't have understood. They were glad to have me home, but I never sat down and talked to them about it. It was just like, 'Okay, I'm home. Here I am.' And I took up where I left off."

He knew, however, that he was a different person from the boy his parents and family had known before he left. "I realized that the experiences in combat had changed me, and I was no longer the little boy they always considered me." In that sense, he echoed the sentiments of other veterans, "feeling different from my family because I had experienced something they had no idea of, and I couldn't tell them about it."

Most of the young men Berne had sent to the service returned there for a while after the war. "But even those of us who had seen combat," Les recalled, "never talked about it among ourselves." For a while, the veterans had a little club above an insurance office in town, where they gathered almost every evening to shoot pool, drink beer, and spend time with other men who at least understood where they had been, what they had seen, and what they had done. Eventually, most of them married or moved on, and the club ran its course.

When Les arrived home on April Fool's Day 1946, all his brothers had already gone back to work at the furniture factory where Jacob worked. "And of course my father, right away, said, 'You've got to go to work.' But I said, 'I just got home, and I ain't going to work.'"

He lived at home with his parents, and his $300 mustering-out pay from the army seemed an enormous sum. For virtually the first time in his life, he did not have to work. Delighted to be home, footloose and free, with a summer of leisure beckoning, he was happier than he had ever been.

He did not want to talk about the war, so his combat experiences were never discussed, but sports remained a constant in his relationship with his brothers. Les's competitive spirit often came to the fore. He said, "Maybe because I was the youngest in a family of five older brothers, I had to be competitive to survive. Otherwise, they'd beat me into the ground."

That first post-war summer found the Habegger brothers competing in Berne's fast-pitch softball league. Five of the brothers formed a family team with four of their Schwartz cousins. Les recalled that the games were hard fought—"and we *had* to win." He alternated between third base and catcher, and served as team manager, and the team won the city championship.

BACK ON THE COURT

Now that Les was back in Indiana, it was almost inevitable that basketball would once again be a part of his life. The American Legion post in Berne had a good team, and Les played for them right after he returned home. They played well enough to reach the Indiana State American Legion Finals. His brothers did not play on the Legion team, but they soon formed an outstanding family team of their own. They each said it was Les's idea, but he maintained that he did not know who had thought of it. "We just got together and we started to play."

They all excelled as athletes. They played against Amateur Athletic Union teams, but under the auspices of an organization called Family Teams. There were many teams comprised of brothers only, and there was even a family team national tournament. Les and his brothers especially relished playing the Clark family team—three sets of twin boys—from Huntington. The Clarks and Habeggers were the best teams in Indiana.

In 1948, the Habegger team was ranked number two in the

country, second only to the Clarks. But they never had the chance to unseat the top-ranked team. Finances had always plagued the Habeggers, and lack of funds kept the team from traveling to the national tournament, which took place in North Carolina that year.

Les loved all things basketball. He listened to games on the radio and went to the home games of the Fort Wayne Zolners, in the Basketball Association of America. Fred Zolner, whose company made pistons for Detroit's automobile industry, owned the team. He eventually moved them to Detroit, where they became the Detroit Pistons of the fledgling National Basketball Association.

When Les's first summer of fun and freedom came to an end, he was still living with his parents. His father sternly advised him again to get a job, so he went to work in the furniture factory. His job as a stringer involved tying springs to furniture frames, and then nailing the twine down with tacks. He kept his mouth full of tacks, rolling them out on his tongue one at a time onto a magnetic hammer head, leaving both hands free to work the twine. He finally decided that "spitting tacks" was not what he wanted to do with his life.

He weighed his present situation: "I was twenty-one years old, had no responsibilities, didn't have a girlfriend, and I wasn't thinking I wanted to get married." He thought back to the times in Hersfeld when he and his fellow soldiers had asked themselves, "What are you going to do when you get home?" He had no idea. He had finished high school with no thought of going on academically. His father had never held any aspirations for his sons, and had never encouraged them to move beyond the confines of Berne, Indiana. But Les had seen more of the world. He had met people from almost every walk of life, and he knew there were other possibilities.

The GI Bill Opens the Door

As Les and other GIs were contemplating their postwar prospects,

WE STILL CALL HIM COACH

the government and veterans organizations were looking at ways to ease their transition from military to civilian life. They did not want to repeat the mistakes that had followed World War I, or to promise rewards they could not deliver. Such mistakes had led to social turmoil in Germany, which allowed the rise of the Nazi party; and, in America, such promises had resulted in the 1932 Bonus Army march on Washington D.C., when disgruntled veterans of World War I marched on the Capitol in an effort to collect on service bonuses granted during the war. After much political wrangling, Congress hammered out a program that combined ideas put forth by both the American Legion and the Roosevelt Administration.

On June 22, 1944, the president signed Public Law 346, the Servicemen's Readjustment Act, better known as the GI Bill of Rights. It provided funding in three primary areas: education and vocational training; unemployment compensation; and guaranteed loans for homes, farms and businesses. Its so-called 52-20 readjustment allowance provided a veteran with twenty dollars a week for up to 52 weeks.

At the time the United States entered the Second World War, high school graduation was still not a universal norm among its teenagers, and attending college was beyond imagining for most. The educational provisions of the GI Bill were hotly debated, and leading college administrators opposed opening admissions to all veterans. One president wanted the colleges to decide who could benefit from a college education, and to say who was worthy. Such objections did not win out, however, and veterans enrolled in droves at colleges across the country.

With the rusty taste of upholstery tacks lingering in his mouth, Les paid a visit to the Veterans Administration (VA) office in Fort Wayne and took a battery of aptitude tests. Decades later, he laughed about the experience and said of the man who administered the tests, "After he graded them, I went back, and I'll never forget what he said: 'One thing is certain. Don't try to go to college, because you'll never make it.' I halfway took his words, but halfway thought, 'The guy's nuts.'" Of one thing he *was* certain, however; he was through with the furniture factory.

Having gained some experience as a dentist's assistant in postwar Hersfeld, Les gave some thought to going to dental school. Because he had maintained sufficient high school grades to be eligible for basketball, he also qualified academically for college. "But I had just turned twenty-one, and was footloose and wanted to 'unwind' after the war." On top of that, the VA's civil servant had told him, "You're never going to go to college, so don't think about going to college. But maybe a trade school."

A town the size of Berne supported one barber shop—a three-chair operation on Main Street that smelled of Wildroot Cream Oil and sported a revolving red-and-white-striped barber pole at the front door. One afternoon, while trimming Les's hair, the shop owner casually asked him whether he would like to become a barber. He went on to say, "I'm president of the Indiana State Barber Board, and I have to travel quite a bit. I need somebody to run the shop while I'm gone. Would you be interested?" Such a likelihood had never crossed Les's mind, but he agreed to think about it.

The VA counselor's words had never completely left him. Barbering was a trade; why not give it a try? As Les said later, "The short of the long is that I said, 'Yeah.'" He had to earn a barber's license, and the GI Bill made it possible for him to enroll that September in the barber college in Indianapolis. He finished the course the following March and returned to run the shop in Berne, even as he served the eighteen-month apprenticeship required for his license.

Les's first stint as a barber was not without its amusing aspects. He told of one mishap that could have cost him a friend. As he honed his gleaming straight razor to a wicked edge and began to shave his buddy's heavily lathered face, a waiting customer distracted him. In an instant, he had nipped a small bit from the top of his friend's ear. He could not believe how profusely an ear—which is primarily cartilage—could bleed. Both he and his victim came close to panic. Les sprinkled talcum powder liberally over the wound, gave his friend a towel to cover the cut, and asked him to sidle out the back door to keep the visual evidence from others in the shop.

By late summer 1948, as the eighteen month apprenticeship neared its end, Les began to think, *This is not what I want to do. This is not what I fought a war for, to stand here and inhale hair all the time.* So, he left the job in the barber shop without having another opportunity lined up first.

"From October 1948 I floated, not sure what in the world I wanted to do. Part of me remembered what the guy at the VA had told me, but the other part was asking, *What am I going to do?* There was nothing for me in Berne. I had worked in the furniture factory, and I didn't want that. I had tried being a barber, and I didn't want that. So what were my options? Well, I could go to college. . . . The guy in the Veteran's Administration, what the hell did he know about me? Okay, so he said I couldn't do it. To heck with that. I decided, *I'm going.*"

Besides that, his eldest brother, Joel, who had worked his way through Ohio State before the war, kept telling him, "You dumb so-and-so, get out of the barber shop and go to college. You need to go to college."

His family still had a great influence in his life. His mother's feelings weighed in many of the decisions he made. Although Rosina had seemed stoic and undemonstrative in the stern, patriarchal world of Les's childhood, she had provided warmth, stability, caring, and compassion to Les. Her principles, beliefs, and strength of conviction stayed with him throughout the nightmarish months of war and occupation. On more than one occasion, what his mother might think had given him pause. Consideration for how his actions would affect her continued after his safe return home. Nothing would have pleased her more than for Les to marry a Mennonite girl from the church in Berne and remain within the family sphere.

During the fun-filled days of the family basketball team, Les's brother Dave and his wife had arranged a blind date for him with the sister of some friends from Decatur. He and Maryann hit it off from the start, and dated regularly for two years. He brought her to the team's games, and she met his parents. Though he never gave her an engagement ring, Les fully intended that he and Maryann would get married, because they had a good relationship.

One problem clouded his sunny horizon—Maryann was a Roman Catholic. Les knew that his mother and father were upset that he was dating a Catholic girl. "During my time in the army," he said, "I had lived with guys from every conceivable religion, state of mind or philosophy, but my parents remained staunch in their negative beliefs about the Catholic Church."

With his mother's consent and cooperation, he invited Maryann home for dinner one Friday night. This was well before Vatican II, so he pointed out that the menu must include fish. Rosina agreed to serve fish, and the meal passed amicably enough. Afterward, Les left to drive Maryann back to Decatur. When he reached the car, he realized he had left his keys on the hall table—something that typically would never happen.

"Providential? I don't know," he said. "Probably. When I ran back in the house to get the keys, I saw my mother, sitting on a chair and just absolutely sobbing. Tears were streaming down her cheeks at the thought that her son was dating and going to marry this Catholic girl. . . . When I saw that, it made me mad, but it also had an effect on me. My better sense said, 'Do I want to enter into a marriage where right off the bat I'm going to have trouble in my family?'"

Just as when he had been impelled to discard the rosary in the snows of Alsace, he knew again that he could not hurt his mother so deeply. He knew there was no way he could marry Maryann.

He "floated" for a while after that, before finally taking Joel's advice and writing to colleges in Indiana and Ohio, seeking admission. Miami of Ohio, just over the border in Oxford and thirty miles from Berne, stood high on his list, but with a flood of veterans applying, they would accept only Ohio residents. Les was left wondering where in Indiana he might decide to go.

In the midst of this internal debate, he dropped in at the American Legion post one night and ran into Max Winterlake, a former basketball opponent who had played for Monroe High School. They relived some memorable high school game highlights before Max told him he was attending Butler University in Indianapolis. He suggested Les join him there and painted a rosy picture of campus life. "I'm in the Sigma Nu fraternity, and if you come I'll get you in the fraternity. We'll have a great time."

Les mulled this prospect for some time, and then contacted Butler. He was accepted, and in February 1949, he moved to Indianapolis and started spring semester as a twenty-four-year-old freshman.

A Life-Changing Witness

Once again, in leaving Berne, he confounded his father, as he had in refusing conscientious objector status in 1943. He had been certain then of his reason—he did not want people to think he was a draft dodger. Now, he knew only that he had to leave town, but he could not really explain why. Decades later, Les recalled that his father had asked why he was leaving. "My father could not understand what was going on in my life. I remember him saying, 'You survived the war, and you came home, and now you're leaving again?' And all I could say to him was, 'You know, Dad, I have to go.' And that's the kind of feeling it was. . . . I just had to go."

Venerable Butler University, founded by abolitionist Ovid Butler, opened in 1855 as North Western Christian University. Butler's Hinkle Fieldhouse, since its opening in 1928, had been the nation's largest basketball arena and home to the Indiana state high school basketball tournament's final round. Indiana roundballers of Les Habegger's generation knew it well.

For some reason, basketball did not figure into Les's experience at Butler, but fraternity life in the Sigma Nu house did. The GI Bill's payment for tuition, books, and a monthly stipend made college possible. Having kept his barber's license current, Les worked in the student union building as a barber. He gained a small measure of notoriety in the spring of 1949 when the Indianapolis newspapers carried a photo of him shaving the beard of the annual junior prom "beard contest" winner. He soon had enough money to buy a car. As he remembered it, "I was an officer in the fraternity, and was doing well. I was on the GI bill, and making money working as a barber, so I bought me a '49 Buick—a nice car—and I was living high."

The high life lasted through summer school 1949 and on through the 1949-50 academic year. As Les neared the end of his sophomore year, a drinking buddy from four years earlier reentered the picture.

Dale Stout, a fellow veteran, older than Les and married, had not been part of the band that gathered regularly at the Berne vets club. "That group," Les said, "was out every night, you know, drinking beer, . . . and we were all single. Dale was married, but he would frequent the taverns and we'd run into him. I got to know Dale very well."

In the spring of 1950, Les received a letter from his mother that changed his life. Perhaps a mother's intuition told Rosina Habegger that her son was seeking a new direction; that he had tired of coming home at two or three o'clock in the morning after drinking all night. In her letter to Les, she wrote, "Dale Stout just became a Christian.

He went to one of these evangelistic meetings in Berne, and he became a Christian."

Les could not believe it: "No way. Not Dale Stout." He reflected on the path he himself had taken since returning from the war. "For three, four years, I was out drinking every night. . . . I didn't murder anybody, but I was out chasing around—and yeah, I was drinking a lot. I really felt, sincerely, at that point in 1950, that I was going to change my life, because that was not the way I wanted to live."

The news in his mother's letter brought Les back to Berne. He looked up Dale Stout and spent a lot of time talking with him. He quizzed Dale about the evangelist who had inspired his conversion to Christianity, and spent night after night asking him about his experience. Dale finally sent him to talk with the evangelist, Harold Walker.

After talking to Harold Walker, Les talked more with Dale, who had a greater influence on him. In the course of all this, he said, "In the summer of 1950, I had a conversion experience," and he accepted Jesus as his personal Savior. Through Dale's influence, he had found a more benign and nurturing God than that depicted by his grandfather during his childhood. "It came as a true revelation to me, after living all those years as an Amish—where everything was religion, religion, religion—and not ever hearing about the love of God. *Never.* Or grace. Or salvation." To hear that God loved him, forgave him, and offered salvation, cast everything in a new light. For the first time in his life, Les knew he was a Christian.

He started changing the way he lived and began thinking seriously about what he wanted to do with his life. Les really did believe in God. He knew that people talked about how God was protective and intervened in situations, and he began to wonder whether he had experienced God's protection and intervention. "I survived the war," he said. "Was that God, or was that just the way it happened? I don't want to argue that. I don't know. But I know how

LEFT: Les Habegger's maternal grandparents, the despotic David Schwartz and Anna Steury Schwartz, ca. 1931.

BELOW: Jacob and Rosina Schwartz Habegger, surrounded by their ten children, spring of 1934. Back row, left to right: Rose, Martha, Eli, Joel, Metta and Selma; middle row: Jesse and Clifton; on either side of their mother, David and Lester.

RIGHT: Monroe Township School teacher, Howard Brandberry's team won the annual Adams County Junior High basketball tournament in 1938. Rosina Habegger sewed proper labels on her sons' team shirts.

Cliff, upper right, and Lester, next to the coach.

LEFT: Les Habegger's status as a noncombatant destined him for service as an army medic, here in full battle dress during basic training at Camp Adair, near Corvallis, Oregon, in late autumn 1943.

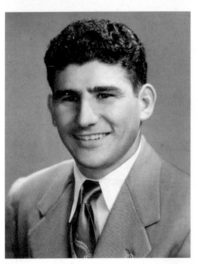

ABOVE: An older and more worldly Les Habegger returned to Indiana in 1946. The ribbons denote service in the European Theater and his commendations.

LEFT: Les Habegger in college, 1954

RIGHT: February 23, 1962, was declared "Les Habegger Appreciation" night at Seattle Pacific. Friends and alumni of the college presented Les and Anne with a new, bright red Chevrolet; modesty prompted the proud owners to trade for a more staid blue model.

LEFT: Falcons in action in the 1964-65 Division II NCAA finals: Dick Smith, number 14; John Crow, number 24; Howard Heppner, number 40, and Dave Rumppe, partially obscured by Heppner's elbow.

ABOVE: Seattle Pacific Varsity, 1965, winner of the Division II NCAA Pacific Coast Regional Championship.

Left to right, standing: coach Les Habegger, John Crow, Gary Habegger, Gary Carnevali, Grant Gullberg, Terry Fein, Dan Petticord, Dick Smith, Howard Heppner, Mel Gimmaka, Bill Hill, Dave Rumppe, Dave Moffitt, and assistant coach Roland K. Halle; kneeling: team manager Dan Dungan, trainer Rick Hoverson, and assistant coach David Wortman.

ABOVE: Rosina Habegger, a frequent Seattle visitor, took great pride in Les's success. Here he explains some of the game's fine point to his mother while wife Anne smiles happily at the floor action, ca., 1965.

ABOVE: An intense coach Habegger follows the action at a 1968 home game, joined by assistant coach Loren Miller; number 44 on the bench is Seattle Pacific's All-American Bill Yeager.

ABOVE: 1979 NBA Western Conference All-Star team. Left to right, standing: trainer Bill Jones, Otis Birdsong, Walter Davis, Dennis Johnson, David Thompson, Paul Westphal, and assistant coach Les Habegger; seated: George McGinnis, Jack Sikma, Kareem Abdul-Jabbar, coach Lenny Wilkens, Artis Gilmore, Maurice Lucas, and Marques Johnson.

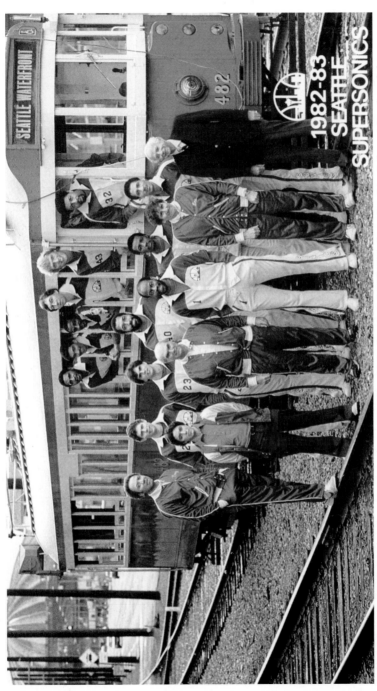

ABOVE: Personnel had changed, but the Sonics were still riding high after their 1979 NBA championship. Left to right, aboard the car: Lonnie Shelton, Mark Radford, David Thompson, Steve Hawes, Jack Sikma, and Fred Brown; back row standing: coach Lenny Wilkens, John Greig, Danny Vranes, James Donaldson, Gregory Kelser, and Phil Smith; front row: equipment manager Scott Alstad, trainer Frank Furtado, Gus Williams, assistant coach Les Habegger, and president, Zollie Volchok. (photo by Bob Peterson)

LEFT: An exuberant Les Habegger responds to the Seattle crowd during a downtown celebration parade following the SuperSonics win over the Washington Bullets for the 1979 NBA title.

ABOVE: Former Seattle SuperSonics founding owner Sam Schulman (center), head coach Lenny Wilkens (left), and assistant coach Les Habegger formed a winning combination that brought Seattle its only NBA title in franchise history.

ABOVE: No remote, sedentary bench coach, Les Habegger took to the court with his multilingual team, the Bundesliga's Steiner-Bayreuth, ca. 1989.

ABOVE: Celebrating the final victory in Europe's Pokal finals, 1989. Les's post-game interviews in fluent "Switzerdeutch" had helped make him a star and a legend in the Bundesliga.

I felt at the time—I did come home safe and sound. God protected me—and my mom thought that too." He had reached the point where he knew God must have some further purpose for him.

He had planned to return to Butler for fall semester, but Walker, the evangelist, had told him, "You can't go back there. You can't go back to the fraternity. . . it's not a Christian organization." Les had enjoyed the university life enormously, but taking Walker's advice to heart, he resigned from Sigma Nu and sold the Buick, his pride and joy.

A short time later, he again did as Walker advised. He wrote to the Northwest Schools in Minneapolis, whose president, a young Billy Graham, was on his way to becoming a force in the spiritual life of the nation. Les had at first balked at the suggestion, saying, "I don't want to be a preacher." But Walker had assured him. "It's a good school. . . . It's not accredited, but it doesn't make any difference." Despite his reservations, Les applied and was accepted. At the end of August 1950, his "best buddy in Berne" drove him to Minneapolis.

CHAPTER SEVEN

WIDENING HORIZONS

When Les arrived in Minneapolis for fall semester 1950, America was experiencing a flood of religious revivals. With a strong desire to replant their roots, returned veterans were among those searching for new directions—and many turned to religion to find them.

During the 1950s, membership at churches and synagogues reached an all-time high. Religious books topped the best seller lists—from the academic writings of theologians Paul Tillich and Reinhold Niebuhr to popular works such as Rabbi Joshua Loth Liebman's *Peace of Mind* and Norman Vincent Peale's *The Power of Positive Thinking*. The new postwar medium of television brought such superstars as Bishop Fulton J. Sheen and evangelist Billy Graham into the nation's living rooms. There was renewed interest in fundamentalism and evangelicalism; their growth and popularity were seen in such movements as Youth for Christ and the Young Life organization. Traveling teams of evangelists fueled the interest in revivalism, and Billy Graham's revival meetings were drawing tens of thousands.

Graham struck a chord with Americans seeking salvation. He once stated that Where did I come from? Why am I here? and Where am I going? were among the most profound questions ever asked. Les himself was wrestling with such questions when he enrolled at the Northwestern Schools.

FINDING THE RIGHT TRACK

The return of fundamentalism to the forefront of America's religious life had been aided by the founding of scores of Bible colleges nationwide during the 1930s and 1940s. In 1935, Dr. William Bell Riley, longtime pastor of First Baptist Church of Minneapolis, oversaw the opening of Northwestern Theological Seminary, with a student body that numbered forty-seven. By 1944, President Riley's Northwestern Schools had grown to include a four-year liberal arts college. Before Dr. Riley died in 1947, he had appointed Billy Graham as his successor. In 1948, the school acquired its first gymnasium, which greatly benefited its growing sports program. The following year, it bought radio station KTIS and began to focus on use of the media.

In the fall of 1950, the new gymnasium provided one positive element in Les's stay in Minneapolis. He went out for the basketball team and made the school's starting five. The school's lack of accreditation had bothered him from the beginning, and he discovered that Northwestern's status as a Bible college meant its curriculum was dominated by study of the Scriptures. He now found himself, a twenty-six-year-old war veteran among teenagers, continuing to wonder about his decision to enroll. He remembered thinking, "I don't know—this doesn't quite ring true."

He found a kindred soul in Jack Kornegay, a fellow veteran from South Carolina, and they became close friends. When Jack, who shared Les's reservations about Northwestern College, told him he was leaving to attend Wheaton College in Illinois, Les decided to apply to Wheaton as well. Les had heard positive things about the four-year, Christian liberal arts college, but Wheaton had already reached its enrollment capacity for the 1951-52 academic year, so Les spent another year in Minneapolis.

Known as "the Fundamentalist Harvard," Wheaton stood virtually unrivaled atop the academic list of Christian colleges. Founded in the mid-nineteenth century, Wheaton reflected the commitment to social reform of its first president, Jonathan Blanchard, a dedicated abolitionist. Very early, the college severed its ties with any denomination, and its nondenominational status appealed to conservative Christian families from all persuasions. Wheaton was also known for its resistance to secular influence, a matter of great importance among Christians who lived according to their understanding of God's biblical commands.

Les enrolled at Wheaton for the 1952 summer term, and discovered the school very much to his liking. "It was a Christian college, but way, way, way different from Northwestern. First of all, it was accredited; students came from every spectrum of the Christian faith; and it wasn't just Bible, Bible, Bible, although we did take some Bible at Wheaton. I enjoyed it, and had a great experience." Wheaton gave him stability, opened up new opportunities, and set him on the career path he would follow.

THE HEIR APPARENT

It is difficult to overstate the importance of basketball to Christian colleges in those days—or to the importance of the colleges to the game. James Naismith, a Canadian physical education teacher, had invented the game in 1891 as an indoor winter replacement for football and baseball at the YMCA International Training School in Springfield, Massachusetts. The excitement of basketball and its challenges to skill and stamina made it an instant hit with the students in Springfield, and they took basketball with them when they graduated and went on to staff YMCA gymnasiums and teach at Christian colleges nationwide. The simplicity and relative economy of the sport appealed to administrators in colleges large and small. Naismith, a theological graduate of McGill University, had created a manly sport that embodied the YMCA's mission to educate students in spirit, mind, and body for leadership in service to humanity.

Wheaton College had embraced basketball at the turn of the twentieth century. Its women's team began intercollegiate competition in 1900, but that program was short-lived. A 1906 faculty ban, which conformed to the prevailing philosophy in women's sports, limited the women to an intramural sports program and kept them from interscholastic competition until 1960.

Men's basketball at Wheaton, which began in 1901, had prospered and grown in popularity over the next five decades. By the time Les brought his superior basketball skills to Wheaton at the beginning of a winning era under Coach Lee Pfund, "Alumni Gym was packed to the window sills" for home games, according to the *Tower*, the school's yearbook. Les was a guard on the team, which competed at the NAIA level in the Collegiate Conference of Illinois. The CCI included schools such as Illinois Wesleyan, Augustana, and Lake Forest.

"It was a good conference," Les recalled, "and we had a very, very good team. In fact, my junior year we went undefeated in conference—and then we got beat in the playoffs." Even though the team failed to win the conference his senior year, Les enjoyed his time at Wheaton immensely. He would later find traces of his Wheaton varsity experience in his own philosophy of coaching.

Coach Lee Pfund had been an assistant at Wheaton in both football and basketball during the 1943-44 school year, but baseball was the sport he personally excelled in. A knee injury had made him unfit for military duty, but in 1945 he pitched for Leo Durocher's Brooklyn Dodgers. A devout Christian, Pfund refused to pitch on Sundays, but Les thought that somehow he managed to blend Durocher's "nice guys finish last" creed with his own high principles. He said, "Coach Pfund's philosophy was Leo Durocher's philosophy. He was a psychologist, who would use Durocher's ideas to motivate us." Pfund was hard-nosed and wanted his teams to be winners. He reinforced Les's commitment to preparing to win, which became the bedrock of Les's coaching philosophy.

Bob Baptista, Wheaton's head soccer coach, who doubled as assistant basketball coach, was also Les's landlord. Older veterans frequently chose off-campus housing, rather than life in the dorms. Les was one of six vets who occupied the second story of Bob and Martha Baptista's house and became very close friends. Baptista later recalled Les as popular, but shy and reserved. He said, "Les Habegger and his friend and roommate Jack Kornegay were veterans of life—a leveling factor—and people looked up to them." With his wide range of playing experience, and being an older player, Les served the Wheaton team as almost a "coach on the floor," who could clarify the coaches' instructions for his younger teammates.

Les credited his decision to major in physical education and minor in social studies to Bob Baptista's influence. It seemed a natural fit for Les to combine his athletic ability with the academic discipline of the Wheaton program. His training and experience as a medic also strengthened his interest in physiology and anatomy courses. He excelled in his studies, and his fellow students elected him president of the Physical Education Majors' Club. His professors predicted a bright future for him.

Les recalled being considered "the heir apparent" to earlier graduates who had gone on to work on their master's and doctoral degrees in physical education. He always suspected they had plans for him to return to Wheaton to teach after earning his advanced degrees, but he told them, "I don't want to be a physical education teacher. I want to be a coach."

This conviction stemmed from the change of course that had taken him to Minneapolis four years earlier. He had said, "I'm not a preacher, I don't want to be a preacher, but I want to accomplish what I can accomplish better as a coach. . . . I want to influence young guys, and I want to coach at a Christian college." He did, however, want to earn a master's degree, and one way for him to reach that goal opened up during his senior year.

The basketball coach at Northwestern Schools offered him a job as his assistant. But Les declined, telling him, "I'm going to be twenty-nine years old when I graduate, and I want to get my master's right away. I'll never go back and get it if I start a job someplace."

The coach at Northwestern responded by making Les an offer he could not refuse. He said, "Les, you can do that at the University of Minnesota, and we'll pay your way through graduate school if you'll come and be my assistant." The salary they offered wasn't much, but the chance to earn his master's degree was too good to pass up. So, in the spring of 1954, he moved back to Minneapolis, became the assistant basketball coach, and taught physical education activity classes at Northwestern.

A College Courtship

The work ethic instilled in him at an early age continued to drive Les during his time at Wheaton. He had enough GI Bill benefits left to get him through school, and he continued to make use of his barber's license, as he had done while at Butler. He rented a small space in the basement of a house just off campus and installed a makeshift barber chair. He posted a notebook on the bulletin board in Blanchard Hall, the campus building with the most foot traffic, and anyone wanting a haircut signed in the notebook for an appointment. "After my last class in the afternoon, around one o'clock, I'd go pick up the notebook, and then I'd go and cut hair until basketball practice started around four. That was pretty much my life: study, cut hair, and practice."

He did, however, still find time for a social life. Like many college students in the 1950s, students at Wheaton shared the expectation of getting married soon after graduation, if not before. As Les recalled, "The feeling on campus at Wheaton when you got to your senior year—well, you'd better get yourself a wife. This was a Christian college, and you had better find a girl you would want to marry." The student body at the time numbered about fifteen hundred. Les had a wide circle of friends and acquaintances, and had dated a number of girls. During his senior year, he met Anne Juul.

He had been awake enough in his 8:00 a.m. religion class to notice an attractive, petite blonde classmate with the looks of a homecoming queen. He enlisted another young woman, a fellow physical education major, to introduce him to her. Years later, Anne had forgotten where they went on their first date, but she did remember one thing: "It was snowing and I put snow down his back. I thought, 'Oh well, I can say good-bye to *him* because I've done that now,' but he threw snow at me, and I fired back." No one remembers who won the snowball fight, but the skirmish marked the beginning of Les's and Anne's courtship.

One thing is certain: their first date did not include a movie. Both Les and Anne remembered Wheaton's strict code for social behavior, which required attendance at daily chapel in the morning, and a ten o'clock curfew at night. Drinking, card playing, dancing, and the like were strictly taboo; and Anne recalled signing a pledge that included a ban on moviegoing, which she thought those raised in a less fundamentalist environment might have resisted. She later mused, "I bought into a lot of the don'ts, which I would certainly argue with today, but at that time I just thought it was what went along with being at Wheaton." She had been raised a Methodist, but as a young adult had affiliated with Emmanuel Covenant Church in Chicago.

Anne was born in Evanston, Illinois, one of three sisters. Her "very Norwegian" parents, Reidar and Anna Juul, moved the family to Glenview when Anne was about seven years old. She attended Niles Township High School in Skokie and graduated in 1949. After her sophomore year at Bradley University in Peoria, she returned home to find a summer job. She was working her way through school, and had run out of money.

Her route to Wheaton opened up that summer. She met a young woman who was active in Young Life, and she, too, became involved. She went to both Frontier Ranch and Star Ranch, and was assigned to work with George Sheffer, a Young Life area director who lived in Wheaton.

Another Young Life friend suggested she go to Wheaton College, and Anne enrolled for fall semester in 1953 as a part-time student. Still needing to work, she recalled, "I got a job at the telephone company there, being an information operator, which is what provided my income until I graduated." Her life at Wheaton included a good job and good places to live. She, too, turned down dorm life, and was one of several college girls who lived in the Sheffers' home.

After majoring in art at Bradley, she changed to education at Wheaton, but kept art as her minor. This proved to be a good combination that allowed her to pursue a teaching career. Her schedule left little time for extracurricular activities. She worked up to thirty hours a week, and carried a full class load of fifteen credits. The courses were solid and demanding, and she laughingly recalled, "I had some courses that were hard for me, and one was, of all things, Bible."

Coach Bob Baptista later became Wheaton's vice president for academic affairs. He believed that, in addition to being a teacher and a researcher, every faculty member should also be "a counselor and guide to students; a role model of Christian maturity." The Baptistas had certainly been role models for Les, who, though he was just a year or two younger, often consulted them on matters ranging from academic and professional to social and personal. Bob and Martha were a tremendous influence in his life, both when he was a student and afterward.

In the Baptista household, Les had seen that a committed coach could also have an intact family, and he thought, *That's not a bad life.* When Bob's coaching duties took him away from Wheaton, as they often did, Martha provided much of the advice and counsel Les sought as he and Anne continued to date after the snowball encounter. Martha was "cautiously positive" about the couple's courtship

When Les moved to Minneapolis to study for his master's degree and coach at Northwestern College, he continued his relationship with Anne by correspondence while she finished her degree at Wheaton. During that year, they each visited the other's home and weathered the inevitable scrutiny of the families. Les found his future father-in-law to be a quiet man, who probably did not consider any young man worthy of his daughters.

Anne recalled that when she visited the Habeggers in Berne, she found the family to be "just as nice as could be. I went down to see his family—so many of them lived around Berne—and I remember them all coming over, and feeling like I was really getting a once-over from everybody." Of Rosina, she said, "Oh, she was adorable. She had living skills—people skills. She did not have a formal education—only sixth grade in the Amish school. But I always thought, 'Boy, that lady has it figured out.' She knew how to function within that society, and she was jolly and good natured." Jacob, on the other hand, was far less outgoing. He stayed on the fringes of the family gatherings. But when "one thing led to another" and Les proposed to Anne, Jacob and most of the family traveled to Chicago for the wedding.

TYING THE KNOT

August 20, 1955, saw the thermometer in Chicago reach triple digits—105 degrees. The sanctuary at Emanuel Covenant Church had no air-conditioning. The wedding party included the bride's two sisters and Janet Normal, her maid of honor, who remained a lifelong friend. Two of the groom's brothers ushered, and Jack Kornegay served as Les's best man.

The newlyweds spent a short honeymoon in northern Minnesota's signature ten thousand lakes country. They made their first home in Minneapolis, and focused their first year together on their careers.

The University of Minnesota enjoyed a postwar golden age in the mid-1950s. The huge enrollment bulge of veterans had diminished somewhat by the time Les and Anne went apartment hunting, but they still found something of a housing shortage.

They paid fifty dollars a month to rent a small upstairs apartment in a private home. "It was an old house," Anne said, "and everything creaked." Their landlady had converted the space into a living room, kitchen, and bedroom. Housekeeping was pretty rudimentary, and their job demands kept socializing to a minimum. Anne laughed when she remembered a time they had company. "The kitchen was full of dishes, so I shoved them all in a dishpan and stuck it in the oven—and, of course, forgot. When I turned on the oven the next time—well, that was fun!"

Leisure time and money were both in short supply as the newlyweds focused on their work. Anne taught at the Thor Thorson School, in a Minneapolis suburb, and Les coached at Northwestern while studying at the university. Starting salaries for teachers were far from generous, and Les recalled he was "getting a pittance."

Anne remembered, "I had thirty-six second graders, and I was fresh—as green as the grass. I'm telling you, I was just as green as the grass. I always had to study and be prepared." Les found himself immersed in coaching, class work, and research. They owned an old Chevrolet, so they did drive down occasionally to visit family. They never managed it during school time, but at Christmas break they went to both Chicago and Berne.

At that time, physical education graduate programs at universities in the Midwest, including Minnesota, emphasized standardization and testing, with a particular focus on statistical measurement. Les thought those classes were interesting, but not especially relevant to his coaching ambitions. He soon had his fill of standard deviation, median, mean, and test construction. His thesis bore one of those tediously descriptive titles: "Adaptive Physical Education Programs in the High Schools in the State of Minnesota." He found the study thought-provoking, especially when he discovered that none of the schools had a special education program, thus relegating students with physical limitations to "study hall."

The required courses in counseling and psychology of learning were taught by inspiring and demanding professors, and here Les found his greatest satisfaction. He did a lot of work in those two areas, and his research papers came back with encouraging notations such as "Excellent work. Well thought out." He recalled his Wheaton experience as "fabulous," but the graduate work was more challenging. "What I digested both in physical education and guidance and counseling—all the reading—I just enjoyed it so much!"

His research papers on the role of a counselor contain kernels of insight that would later be absorbed into his philosophy of coaching. Among them were building trust, evaluating activity so as to improve future work, and helping the individual reach his optimum development. Les saw great possibilities for accomplishing positive things, and at one point he said to himself, "Okay, then, I'll be a counselor in high school."

But something else he had written about the counselor's vocation must have given him pause: "Can we play or act a role that doesn't fit us and still be effective?" His own skill and experience made the coaching role a perfect fit. He felt that his desire to be "more than just an ordinary guy," but one who could work to influence young men, had been a call from God. So, during his last year of graduate school, he searched for coaching vacancies at Christian colleges.

AN OPPORTUNITY OUT WEST

The placement office files at Northwestern Schools yielded a number of possible opportunities at colleges in New York, California, and Illinois—and one he had never heard of: Seattle Pacific College in Washington. He mailed out a battery of letters, and Seattle Pacific responded with word that they were looking for an assistant basketball coach and someone to teach in the physical education department. The thought of a school in the Pacific Northwest intrigued him. Oregon's constant rain had been erased from his memory by the hot summer of 1944 in Missouri, so he told Anne that Seattle Pacific might be a good thing. "Let's go out and see what it's like. We don't know. I like the West Coast; it has great weather." He thought perhaps they could go to Seattle for a couple of years, and then move back to the Midwest and settle down closer to family.

Anne had known that when Les finished his degree they would make a change, but she had not agonized over it. She felt no strong attachment to the school where she taught. "I just figured you go where the husband goes."

In the spring of 1956, Les and Anne drove to Seattle to investigate the possibilities. "It was a nice trip out," Anne remembered. "I mean, it was like a honeymoon, practically."

The nation's postwar economy was booming, fueled in large part by a growing demand for automobiles. In Seattle, the pressure for new cars caused dealers to fill their showrooms with new models sent from the overstock of their counterparts in the Midwest. The Habeggers contacted a dealership in Minneapolis that had a car destined for Seattle, and drove it out for them. Les said, "They paid for the gas. They didn't pay us any money for driving, but they paid the gas." Neither Les nor Anne could remember the make or model of the car, or where they delivered it in Seattle.

The two or three days they spent on the Seattle Pacific campus were far more memorable. Les's correspondence had been with Dr. C. Hoyt Watson, SPC's president, who apparently had not shared news of their visit with the school's athletic director, Ken Foreman. They met Foreman and his wife on their arrival. Anne said, "We were totally unexpected, but they were very gracious and invited us to go get fish and chips with them." "We piled into their station wagon—us, the Foremans, and their three children—and went for supper. I remember sitting there, having fish and chips, and thinking, *What an adventure*. And they were so nice."

Ken Foreman arranged for them to stay in one of the dormitories. "It was all very basic," Les said, "and they had us over to meet their good friends. The whole point was to get their opinion, and their okay, so that was interesting."

Les concentrated on the professional possibilities during their stay in Seattle. He met with President Watson and spent considerable time with Ken Foreman. He had the opportunity to survey the physical education instructional program, as well as the varsity basketball situation. The college's intercollegiate record and participation at that point left much to be desired, but Les saw potential as well as a challenge. He and Anne left the Puget Sound area with a positive feeling about Seattle Pacific.

Their return trip to Minneapolis underscored the lack of

money that had always plagued them. As Les recalled, "We took the Greyhound bus, because we had no money—just enough for the Greyhound ticket back. I'll never forget. We got to Fargo, North Dakota, and we had just enough money to split a grilled cheese sandwich at the bus station. When we got to Minneapolis, we had whatever the pay phones cost in those days, a dime or something. So we called our friends and said, 'We're at the bus station and we have no money, but we're getting a taxi. Will you pay the cab driver when we get there?'" All in all, they had had a great trip, and further correspondence with President Watson soon followed.

As Les neared the end of his last semester of graduate school, Seattle Pacific offered him a job as an instructor, at a salary of $3300. At that point, he had received only one other possible job offer—to teach in a high school in Michigan. Even with nothing more than that, and with his determination to coach and teach at the college level, Les said, "When Dr. Watson sent me this offer letter, I had the nerve to write back and say, 'I can't come for $3300.'"

The year before, the college had purchased five hundred acres at Fort Casey on Whidbey Island in Puget Sound. The historic old fort predated the Spanish-American War, and when the federal government declared it surplus, SPC saw it as a perfect site for both educational and recreational use. President Watson took note of Les's graduate work in guidance and counseling and revised the offer to include responsibilities at Camp Casey, the rank of instructor at the college, and a salary that totaled $3900. Les accepted, and later said, "I never spent a day working at Camp Casey. He put it in so he could pay me more money."

The terms of that first contract were demanding enough, without adding more duties on the island. He was named as assistant athletic coach and supervisor of camp counselors, which called for him to participate in the "usual committee and extracurricular work." He would teach in the instructional physical education program; coach the junior varsity basketball and varsity baseball teams; carry a "real responsibility" for the intramural program; supervise outdoor education cadet counselors, in cooperation with the public schools; and possibly "render assistance" to the director of student guidance. The contract included college-funded participation in its group insurance and hospitalization plans, and matching contributions to the faculty retirement plan. It also promised payment of $250 toward their moving expenses.

Before making a final decision to accept the Seattle Pacific offer, Les received conflicting advice from his Wheaton connections. As luck would have it, Dr. V. Raymond Edman, Wheaton College's president, delivered the Northwestern Schools commencement address that spring, and Les was selected to escort him during his stay in Minneapolis. Les knew Dr. Edman from his days at Wheaton, so as they drove to the train station to leave, Les did not hesitate to ask his opinion. He later recalled Dr. Edman's exact words: "My spirit tells me that you should go to Seattle Pacific." "Given my respect and admiration for Dr. Edman, that was part of what convinced me I should go."

When he contacted Bob and Martha Baptista, however, they advised against it because of SPC's affiliation with the conservative Free Methodist denomination. The Baptistas had just completed a sabbatical year of teaching at another Free Methodist college, which they had found very restrictive; Bob thought there might be some restrictions at Seattle Pacific that Les would not like.

Les mulled things over. He knew he wanted to coach, and he knew this was a good opportunity. "Finally," he said later, "I really wanted to do this, so I went anyway."Les and Anne were relieved to have their financial problems settled and the major decision behind them. Only the emotional aspects of leaving the Midwest lay ahead. Anne considered the whole thing as an adventure, but she remembered her father saying, "If you move out there you'll never see us, because we're never coming out.' Well, they were there the next summer—they drove out—and every summer thereafter for years."

For Les, however, the move to the West Coast caused one more break with his family and produced conflicted emotions that never left him. He later said, "I know I disappointed my father. I know I did. Mom never said much, although she had similar feelings. But Mom didn't lay it on you like Dad did. When I left for Seattle Pacific, he said, 'I don't understand. Why are you doing this? Why are you going so far from home?'"

All of Les's brothers and sisters still lived in Berne. "We were all right there together. And there's that ache inside of me today from separating myself from the family." Yet he knew there was nothing there for him. His voice trailed off as he said, "Yeah, I could have stayed in the barber shop, could have stayed in the factory . . ."

Instead, he remained true to his dream of coaching and his desire to be more than ordinary. Seattle Pacific College allowed him to do that and to pursue his desire to help young Christian men toward attaining their full potential.

CHAPTER EIGHT

SEATTLE PACIFIC: THE EARLY YEARS

A disastrous fire had all but destroyed Seattle in 1889, but the city had recovered, rebuilt, and benefited handsomely from the Alaska gold rush of 1897. Its growing population had expanded and spread outward onto the surrounding hills. Early arrivals had already moved onto Queen Anne Hill, just to the north of the city's core. In June 1891, Nils Peterson, a Queen Anne homesteader, donated five acres of land on the lower north slope of the hill to the Free Methodist Church as a location for its Seattle Seminary, a preparatory school.

Since its founding in 1860, Free Methodism had been known for its commitment to education. It established more liberal arts colleges than the size of the denomination would seem to warrant. The "free" in Free Methodism conveys the founders' strong dedication to the abolition of slavery, and it relates to the practice of providing free pews for congregants, which was in direct opposition to the discriminatory custom of renting better-situated pews to better-situated parishioners. Free Methodists sought to return to their spiritual roots and the teachings of Methodism's founder, John

Wesley, but some conservative social restrictions went beyond those of the founder and were carried to an extreme.

The new school in the shadow of Queen Anne Hill offered a strong academic program. A full college curriculum was added in 1910, and the name changed to Seattle Seminary and College. In 1915, it became Seattle Pacific College. Its enrollment had never been large, but the influx of World War II veterans swelled the ranks of students. By 1958, the enrollment had grown to 1,400. This period also saw physical growth on campus, as five new buildings went up, including a new gymnasium—the state-of-the-art Royal Brougham Pavilion. The curriculum expanded to include a school of recreational leadership as part of the physical education program. Through all the growth and change, the college adhered to its themes of "Educating for Effective Christian Living" and "Dedication to Scholarship."

SETTLING IN AND MAKING ADJUSTMENTS

Les and Anne Habegger entered the tight-knit Seattle Pacific community in August 1956. They were put in touch with Vern Archer, an SPC alumnus, who owned apartment buildings not far from campus. Archer had a vacancy—a furnished unit, which the newcomers rented for $75 a month. They had arrived with all their worldly belongings packed in their car. Anne's parents had given them a black-and-white television set; otherwise, their home furnishings were sparse.

Les remembered following a common 1950s practice in equipping the apartment. "I went up to the Safeway on top of Queen Anne Hill and begged some boxes and peach crates, and we made night tables out of the peach crates. We also got some old boxes and made a coffee table, and that was the way we set up shop. I think the apartment had a small dining room table with four chairs, and we lived there for three years."

Their possessions and possibilities for entertaining increased the next summer when Anne's parents made their first trip from Illinois, bringing a complete table service of better dishes.

With their living arrangements settled, the young couple contemplated their status in the new environment, which at the time was quite conservative. Bob and Martha Baptista had shared their recent experience on a very conservative Free Methodist campus, which included a ban on wearing wedding rings, earrings, and makeup. Les and Anne had not sensed such an attitude when they visited SPC that spring, but now they wondered.

Les recalled that Anne asked, "'Do I stop wearing lipstick?' I said, 'No way. This is who we are.'" He later said, "I think Anne at that time was the only faculty spouse who was wearing lipstick and any kind of jewelry."

Anne herself recalled that when she found that she and one faculty member were the only women on campus who wore earrings, she thought *Boy, I better take these off.* "But the other young wives were kind of in the same boat." The Habeggers did find SPC strict in 1956, but the rigid Free Methodist social regulations would soon begin to ease.

On their earlier trip to Seattle in the spring, while Les explored the coaching and teaching opportunities at the college, Anne had done the same with the public schools. She had applied for a job with the Seattle School District, and fall semester 1956 found her teaching second grade at a school in the city's north end. She taught primary grades there for the next three years, and they remained a two-income household.

Public school salaries were not generous, but they surpassed those paid then by Seattle Pacific. Anne recalled, "I made, for my first year teaching here in Seattle, I think it was $3400 for the year, and Les got only a little more with a master's degree at the college. It was like you were a missionary." Les, too, recalled the financial pinch: "If it wasn't for her, we wouldn't have made it. That first year, I supplemented my income by carrying mail at Christmas time."

The young Habeggers settled easily into campus life. "We had fun," Anne recalled of their circle of friends. "And in those days, we'd sit and laugh, and just have the best time."

She also served as adviser to the Falconettes, the campus service club for girls. "I was adviser one year to the cheerleaders, and really went to bat for them, because they bought uniforms that some people frowned on. They thought they were too short, or some goofy thing. So I went to the president—and the girls just loved it that I stood up for them." As the coach's wife, she soon made a hit with Les's players, as well.

As Anne adjusted to the role of faculty wife, Les plunged wholeheartedly into his formidable schedule of teaching, coaching, and extracurricular responsibilities. He met challenges, along with a few surprises, not the least of which was the school's lack of a strong commitment to winning.

The student campus newspaper, *The Falcon*, had editorialized on the subject of competition the year before. The piece led off with the famous Grantland Rice quotation: "When the One Great Scorer comes to mark against your name, he writes not that you won or lost—but how you played the Game." After citing "fair play, honesty, concentration and cleanliness" as virtues an athlete should possess, the writer for *The Falcon* said their goal in intercollegiate athletics was to put "our high standards of sportsmanship into practice and to show forth Christ's teaching and attitudes when meeting an opponent. . . . Winning is important, but when we win, let us win humbly. If we lose, let us lose valiantly with honor." The falcon had been chosen as the school's mascot, because it is a swift, fair, invincible, and noble bird. SPC's athletes were said to know how to lose nobly "as well as win."

Les may or may not have read that piece when he visited the

campus, but he did remember that Dean Philip Ashton had told him, "We don't care whether we win or not; we just want the guys to be good sports." Les also remembered replying, "I think you got the wrong guy. I *do* care about winning." Creating a winning philosophy became a top priority for the athletic program's new hire.

A SURPRISING TURN

As one of only three instructors in the physical education department, as well as being an assistant athletic coach, Les carried an incredibly heavy load. All three instructors, including Ken Foreman the athletic director, taught sports activity classes for the student body of more than one thousand; and they taught all the professional theory classes for the sizable number of physical education majors as well. Golf and volleyball were among the sports Les taught that first year, and his theory classes included Philosophy of Physical Education and Administration of Physical Education in the Public Schools. He also headed the large intramural program on campus.

His coaching duties extended throughout the academic year and heaped the plate even higher. As assistant basketball coach, he led the junior varsity as well, and at season's end he donned his varsity baseball coach's hat. At the end of that first basketball season came the biggest surprise of all—head coach, department chair, and athletic director Ken Foreman resigned. A national NCAA gymnastics champion from the University of Southern California, Foreman was returning to his alma mater to study for a doctoral degree.

Les had never been told that Foreman planned to leave, and his plate came near to spilling over when he was named to succeed Foreman as both varsity basketball coach and athletic director, in addition to all his other responsibilities.

Soon after Les arrived on campus, *The Falcon* ran an article quoting him as saying, "SPC has got something, and I want to back it." He said he was pleased with the facilities and the athletic setup, and he considered Royal Brougham Pavilion one of the best gymnasiums he had ever seen. Bits of his philosophy came through as well, when he said that basketball helped to develop a man for the future, and that he considered sports just another way of presenting Christ to the people. He was pleased that SPC had an emphasis on spiritual things and Christ. He found the school's motto, "Youth Facing Life with Christ," very fitting, and said he was proud to be a part of SPC.

Taking the Reins

In 1956, collegiate basketball in Seattle enjoyed lofty status in the press and among the city's sports enthusiasts. At the city's two NCAA Division I schools, Coach Tippy Dye's University of Washington Huskies included All-American Doug Smart; and at Seattle University, the rising star of All-American and future NBA Hall of Famer Elgin Baylor shone brightly for coach John Castelloni. At much smaller Seattle Pacific, which at the time played in the National Association of Intercollegiate Athletics (NAIA), Ken Foreman welcomed the return of Orville and Loren Anderson for another season.

The Andersons had played on a team that compiled a 15-12 won/loss record the year before, the school's first winning season since 1948. The Seattle Pacific basketball scene had been one of peaks and valleys, and a record of 11-15 during Les's first year on campus signaled another downturn. But when the time came to choose Ken Foreman's replacement as head coach in the spring of 1957, Les was an obvious leading candidate.

He met the selection committee's criteria. He was dedicated to the ideals of Christian education, held an advanced degree, and had demonstrated his coaching ability. For his part, Les found the decision to accept the job fairly easy. He said, "There are great possibilities here to go with the progress that has already been made. . . . I see a brilliant future and want to be part of it." He restated his belief in the character-building value of athletics in Christian colleges, and emphasized that athletics can be a powerful witness for Christ. He also said that athletics could provide good publicity for the college.

Profound optimism had not been one of the requirements for the head coaching position, but in his first season at the helm, Les displayed it in abundance. He drove the team hard, drilled them endlessly on fundamentals, and emphasized conditioning and defense. *The Falcon* reported that bad shots and bruises had marked the team tryouts, and soon dubbed the Habegger 3-2 type of offense "race horse basketball." With three guards, two forwards, and no true center, it was hoped that speed and conditioning would allow SPC to "run the opposition to death."

Years later, that first season remained burned in Les's memory—six wins and twenty losses. He later recalled, "The first game we won—I don't think was until January—they carried me off the floor." Ever the optimist, Les chalked up their problems to inexperience in his recap of the season: "As far as I'm concerned, the season was a success. . . . I can think of seven games we should have won. We were ahead at crucial times and then lost the game mainly because of one thing—inexperience."

The Habegger Era Begins in Earnest

Gradually, Seattle Pacific basketball began to take on a Habegger tone and to reflect his insistence on conditioning and preparation. Les greeted the next season with no predictions, but said, "I'm sure we'll have a more impressive record this year." Starting on the road with two losses, the team returned to win its home opener in Royal

Brougham Pavilion against St. Martin's College, and they went on to compile a record of eleven wins and fourteen losses.

Les launched his third season at the helm with a team retreat at Camp Casey. "The purpose," he said, "was to build group solidarity and unity and to prepare us physically and spiritually for the challenges that lay ahead."

By early January 1960, their record was 9-6. A photo in *The Falcon* showed a joyous team above a caption that read, "Falcons in Victory: Togetherness Triumphs." By February, the paper proclaimed support for the team "at a level unprecedented for the school," and traced the success to team unity. The article cited the team motto—Philippians 4:13—chosen before the season began: "I can do all things through Christ which strengtheneth me," and added, "Teamwork has been the key. . . . Every win has been a team win and every loss has been a team loss."

One Sunday evening in February, in the middle of their run of victories, the basketball team met its commitment to the wider community at a newly established church in the Seattle suburb of Lynnwood. *The Falcon* reported that Les spoke and team members provided "special music and personal testimonies."

The Falcons finished the 1960 season with a record of seventeen wins and ten losses. The Habegger era at Seattle Pacific had begun in earnest. Now playing his system and reflecting his philosophy and will to win, Les's teams would not have another losing season. He made Seattle Pacific a regional basketball powerhouse and garnered national respect as well. That October, *The Falcon* reported that Seattle Pacific had recently joined the small-college National Collegiate Athletic Association, thus making it possible to go on to either NAIA or NCAA playoffs.

Les himself gained a sterling reputation, both on and beyond the campus. Seattle Pacific started each academic year with a faculty retreat at Camp Casey. Grounded in academics, it served to bond the faculty as a family. One of Les's faculty colleagues recalled that this gathering was so important that "you had to be on your death bed to miss it." He went on to say, "Les was very much a presence at the faculty retreats." His interests extended beyond athletics, and he bridged the divide between departments with ease. He became a major player at the informal faculty gatherings for coffee in the student union.

The fan growth and unprecedented enthusiasm for basketball reflected not only the power of a winning team to attract attention, but also that things were gradually changing. When the Habeggers arrived at Seattle Pacific, there was a strong sense of mission and a feeling of "family" that prevailed. In addition to training for missions worldwide, the school's role was seen as bringing a Christian witness to the wider community through its programs in music and drama—and athletics now as well. Anne's description of the salary scale as comparable to that of a missionary organization captured precisely the period's expectation that you worked in a sacrificial role and did not expect to be paid a salary comparable to that in a nonsectarian school.

The conviction that teachers served the students and went above and beyond the call of duty at great sacrifice slowly gave way, hastened by faculty retirements. Replacements for the old guard were young and more liberal, newly minted PhDs from secular universities. The youth movement was accompanied by changes in the president's office. In 1959, the long-serving Dr. Watson gave way to Dr. C. Dorr Demaray, the highly respected senior minister of Seattle's First Free Methodist Church. In the spring of 1968, the trustees chose Dr. David McKenna, who came from Spring Arbor College in Michigan to lead SPC through a period of growth and change and into university status. Although the athletic department and its programs received strong support from both administrations, funding remained a major difficulty and a source of frustration.

The problem of providing team transportation illustrates what an albatross the budget was for Les, beginning with his first year as head coach. The team always traveled to away games in private automobiles. Throughout Les's twenty-year tenure, there was never a college van for team use. Les and his assistant coach drove their own cars to games in Ellensburg, Bellingham, or Spokane. Occasionally, in the early years, they called on boosters, parents, and players who had cars to drive as well. Because Les stretched his travel funds to cover meals and lodging, he often took less reimbursement for gasoline—sometimes even paying for it himself to save travel money so the team could eat.

The money crunch was not alleviated by gate receipts. "When I first started," Les said, "my first year, we sold two season tickets." There was no money to staff the ticket window for home games, so Les relied on student volunteers. Opening the ticket window and lending the students a hand started a new routine for Les: After his pre-game talk with the players in the dressing room, he would go back and sell tickets until the game started.

The Falcon Club soon became involved and helped to ease the financial strain. The club had been started by Ken Foreman and several alumni boosters. During his first year as head coach, Les worked with Dr. Marvin Wallace, a prominent local physician, to increase the club's potential for fund-raising. A Seattle Pacific alumnus and close friend of the college's presidents, Dr. Wallace served as a trustee of the college and befriended its athletic programs. As Les recalled, Dr. Wallace said, "For every basketball season ticket that people buy, I will double it." That year, they sold only two. But the next year, a few more were sold, and gradually over the years they built it up. Success fueled the growth of both the club and the crowds at Brougham Pavilion. By the end of the 1962 season, it was standing room only.

Building a Winning Program

When the 1960 season closed on a winning note, *The Falcon* had proclaimed that "prospects for next season look very bright," even though Les predicted it would be one of the toughest seasons they had ever faced. Their schedule included strong nonconference teams from the University of Washington and Seattle University. Still, Les felt that with his players' good speed and scoring ability, and even with an expected height disadvantage, they would make it into the district playoffs and possibly further.

The 1960-61 starting team emerged from weeks of rugged and competitive training that culminated in the now traditional team retreat at Camp Casey. This year, it featured talks by Earl Palmer, then youth minister at Seattle's University Presbyterian Church, who challenged the players to be proud to represent a Christian college in intercollegiate athletics. In spite of a slow start, the Falcons finished the regular season with six wins in their last seven games. They lost to Whitworth College in the district tournament finals in Spokane, but finished the year with a winning record of 15-13. Their record for 1961-62 was even better—twenty wins against only seven losses.

Their 20-7 season brought them an invitation to the 1962 NCAA tournament. Les recalled, "I really wanted to go to the NCAA." He took his case to President Demaray, who was really a good guy in Les's book. He told the president, "We've got an offer to play in the NCAA playoffs. We've got a good team. I really want to do this. But if we do, the NAIA will put us on probation, or may kick us out." He recalled that Dr. Demaray did not hesitate, but told him, "If that's what you want to do, then do it." As for any repercussions from the NAIA, he said, "Let me handle that."

Seattle Pacific accepted the NCAA bid in 1962, losing to the eventual winner, Sacramento State, in the opening round, but upsetting Fresno State in the consolation round to finish third.

Seattle Pacific remained in the NCAA, and postseason play came to be expected of Les's teams. Winning seasons also made SPC a more attractive place for recruiting strong player prospects.

Recruiting was part of the incredible load that Les had carried for three years while Ken Foreman studied for his doctorate in California. Fortunately, in October 1960, Foreman returned to Seattle Pacific, and he and Les redrew the lines of responsibility. Foreman assumed chairmanship of the physical education program, and Les continued as athletic director.

The meager Seattle Pacific athletic budget put recruiting very low on the list of priorities. Les recalled that, in the early years, "If I took a recruiting trip, it was out of my own pocket. In my own car." He drove from British Columbia down to southern Washington to visit families whose talented sons he wanted to bring to Seattle Pacific. Early on, the nature of the college limited recruiting somewhat, but Les said, "Many guys wanted to come to a Christian college, or their parents wanted them to come, so I got a lot of players that way. . . . I got players initially just by writing letters." He could also be found at high school tournaments.

"I'd go to the state tournaments, and I'd look at players I thought I'd like, and then I'd write them letters. And of course, it was like being a salesman—out of every five letters, you might get three back, or something like that, and that's kind of how it went."

The academic rigor of the college focused his search around a pool of scholar athletes. The budget made it virtually impossible to offer scholarships, no matter how promising the player; but as time went on and winning became a tradition, Les began to hear from more people interested in a small school. "They wanted to play at SPC because we had a good program and it was local."

In addition to the financial and academic aspects of a school, the coach's philosophy was fundamental in recruiting. Since childhood, Les had been a fierce competitor, and he sought players who displayed the same determination. He had gained a reputation as a hard-nosed, driving coach who demanded conditioning and total preparation, and he always played to win. While a competitive and aggressive approach to sports might appear to some as antithetical to Christian values, there were no contradictions in the mind of Les Habegger.

He viewed the game of basketball as life itself; hence his philosophy of coaching was the same as his philosophy of life: "Whatever is worth doing is worth doing well." Though winning was important, it was not necessarily the most important thing—but preparing to win *was* important. "Because life demands our best," Les said, "anything less is failure. Losses will come, each with its own lesson. But if a loss comes as a result of lackadaisical effort, indifference, or inadequate preparation, it's unforgivable."

For Les, coaching presented the opportunity to realize his goal of helping young men to lead fulfilling lives as Christians. He maintained that, for college players, basketball should be used as a means to an end; as an avenue for social, physical, emotional, and spiritual maturation. He took his responsibility seriously. "If all I teach these guys is how to put the ball through the basket more times than our opponents, I have indeed failed as a teacher of young men. The kind of people these athletes become is important to me."

Dedication to the principles of preparation and execution, and his mastery of the X's and O's, produced winning records and player loyalty. Near the end of the successful 1962 season, the *Seattle Times* quoted one of his players: "Coach has that certain quality that cannot be defined. It's something that makes us want to play our hearts out for him."

In his first six years in Seattle, Les had turned the basketball program around. As Harland Beery, director of the SPC news bureau, saw it, Seattle Pacific had moved out of its niche on the religion page to a place on the front page and the sports page. Seattle's two daily papers had gone from simply having someone call in the score after a home game to assigning a regular beat writer to cover the Falcons. Winning had brought far-flung alumni support on road trips as well. When the Falcons traveled south and defeated Pasadena College in January 1962, many alums were on hand to cheer them on. The college publicity office deemed the road trip "a great success, both in results and publicity received."

Branching Out at Camp Casey

Les's accomplishments did not go unnoticed by President Demaray. The contract he offered Les for the 1962-63 year was for $6500, an annual increase of $1000. Les's success at Seattle Pacific registered on other campuses as well, and job offers came his way from other schools, including Westmont College in Santa Barbara. Nowhere did the move into postseason play resonate stronger and more happily than among SPC sports boosters. Men who had driven the team to an untold number of games, and others, such as Marvin Wallace and Vern Archer, who had contributed to the school in countless other ways, did not want to see Les leave. On December 16, 1962, Dr. Wallace loaned Les and Anne $6667 as the down payment for a house with a view on the hill above the campus. Les recalled later, "That's the only way I could buy it—with borrowed money." A home of their own was a strong inducement to stay in Seattle.

Having built his Seattle Pacific program into a success, Les found personal support in the broader community to go along with the solid relationships he had formed in Seattle's college basketball circles. In 1963, those connections merged and gave impetus to an innovative idea—a summer camp for high school players.

Bob Houbregs, the Converse shoe company representative who sold to the SPC program, became Les's good and close friend. Houbregs's name stood atop the list of the city's basketball legends in the 1950s and 1960s. An All-America center, he led the University of Washington Huskies to the Final Four in 1953, and went third overall in the NBA draft that fall as the number one pick of the Atlanta Hawks. Houbregs had played six seasons with the Hawks before an injury forced his retirement.

At that time, Seattle claimed few restaurants of distinction, but The Grove, near Seattle Center and the Space Needle, was one of them. The owner of The Grove, Les Brainerd, was a staunch fan of Huskies basketball and had become a great friend of Bob Houbregs. Brainerd became a Seattle Pacific donor as well, and made The Grove the site of pregame meals for the Falcons. Bob Houbregs and Les often ate lunch at The Grove, and one day during dessert, following the successful 1962 season, they began talking about starting a basketball camp. Brainerd picked up on the conversation. He was interested in the idea, and as Les recalled it, he said, "I'll tell you what. I'll go over with you to the bank, and I'll sign for five thousand dollars to get your camp started."

After the trip to the bank across the street settled the financial end of things, they still needed a place to conduct the camps. That's when Marv Wallace entered the picture. He had earlier talked to Les about Camp Casey and even suggested that he start a sports camp there. In order to bring Les to Seattle in 1956, adding duties at the camp to his contract had allowed President Watson to offer him a better salary, but such responsibilities had never materialized. Les had been to countless retreats there, but now, under President Demaray, Camp Casey offered an extraordinary opportunity.

Les recalled saying to Bob Houbregs, "Hey, we've got Camp Casey. We've got a facility, but we—you and I—will have to build the courts, because there are no courts out there. There's an old gym, but it's too small."

Bob said, "Let's do it."

The $5000 bank loan from Les Brainerd went to build two full-size, outdoor asphalt courts for that first summer of 1963. As the camp succeeded, they built two more, and a decade later they had six.

Marv Wallace brokered a deal with Seattle Pacific, and secured the minimum possible rent for the use of Camp Casey. Les and Bob rented the barracks and the land; but by providing their own cook and provisions, they avoided any food costs charged by the college. Their cook was Bob's mother, who worked in food services with the Seattle school district. "She was a fabulous cook," Les recalled, "and the kids who came to our camp ate like kings."

Ever self-effacing, Les remained in the background and Bob Houbregs became the public face of what may have been the first such summer camp in the country for high school basketball players. The brochures they sent out for the Bob Houbregs Basketball Camp created enormous interest. Houbregs's name was a magnet that drew parents to register their kids for the weeklong sessions that ran throughout the summer.

All the counselors were college basketball players who wanted to spend the summer playing basketball. They received room and board, plus a weekly stipend. Bob and Les did much of the coaching themselves, but they also relied on local high school coaches who wanted to come up and get exposure. "Depending on how many boys we had each week, we'd invite so many high school coaches," Les said.

The camp's first season was a success in every sense of the word. They repaid the loan arranged for them by Les Brainerd and looked to future summers with confidence and enthusiasm. Over time, college coaches from as far away as Tennessee made guest appearances; and after the Seattle Supersonics joined the NBA, Lenny Wilkens, a Sonics icon, joined the parade of stars at the camp on Whidbey Island.

KIDS AND KUDOS

During the early turnaround years at Seattle Pacific, life for Anne Habegger, too, revolved around basketball. With her teaching career and Les's incredibly demanding hours, it was difficult to maintain any kind of domestic schedule during the basketball season. She went to almost all the home games, sharing in the joy of the victories and tolerating her husband's less than benign reaction to the losses. She knew better than anyone that Les Habegger did not like to lose.

In January 1960, life for the Habeggers had added another dimension with the birth of their son, Scott. The Falcons were playing in Nampa, Idaho, when Les got the phone call announcing his son's arrival. Career-oriented working mothers were a rarity in 1960 when Anne returned to teaching; she taught until their second child, Julie, was born. Anne recalled no regrets over quitting her job. "I was so glad, because it tore me up to drop Scott off at a babysitter's on my way to school."

Not long before Julie was born on April 11, 1962, Les and Anne experienced one of the biggest thrills of the early SPC days. The last home game of the season on February 23 was declared "Les Habegger Appreciation Night." In response to a campaign orchestrated by Vern Archer, friends and alumni of the college contributed funds for a car to replace the one Les had literally worn out on behalf of the basketball program. Les later insisted that it was embarrassing, but Anne recalled the evening of ovations and tributes as a high point of their time at the college. At halftime of the game against Southern Oregon, the Habeggers were summoned to center court at Royal Brougham Pavilion. As Anne recalled, "I went out on the floor in my homemade maternity dress, which wasn't all that bad as I look back, and they presented us with keys to a new car." The original gift was a bright red Chevrolet, but the proud new, low-key owners quietly negotiated a trade for a more sedate blue model.

Throughout his first six years at Seattle Pacific, Les had carried a complex load—professor of physical education, athletic director, and head basketball coach. His presence at the morning faculty coffee klatch helped bridge the divide between academics and athletics, and the success of his teams increased faculty attendance at games. With Seattle Pacific now playing in the NCAA, the future looked both bright and challenging. But no one relished a challenge more than Les Habegger.

CHAPTER NINE

CHALLENGES, CHANGE
AND A WINNING TRADITION

The euphoria of the spring of 1962 lasted well into October when Les assembled his varsity for the next season. The Falcons would compile a 16-9 record that year but not progress to the NCAA tournament. They finished the 1963-64 season with seventeen wins against ten losses and returned to postseason play.

A winning record will substantially boost a school's recruiting, and Seattle Pacific benefited from its team's success. Les continued his rounds of the high school tournaments and followed up leads from fans and alumni. The college athletic budget remained a problem, but he made the available funds go as far as possible. When some faculty members criticized athletic department expenses, he countered by pointing out that Seattle Pacific got a lot of notoriety from its basketball program.

The team's consistently good records played positively in the press, and brought inquiries and campus visits from prospective players. Les said, "Now people wanted to come and play here; they wanted the small school." He could give top-tier prospects full tuition scholarships, and some others received half tuition. For other players, he had to find more innovative ways to get them to choose SPC, such as telling them, "I'll give you a hundred dollars, or a hundred and fifty, or you can sweep the gym floor after practice and I'll pay you that way." In Les's twenty years at SPC, only two players received a full ride, tuition, room and board scholarship—Howard Heppner, who came in 1963, and Jim Ballard, who played on the strong teams of the early 1970s.

The investment in the 6'5" Heppner paid enormous dividends. He came to SPC from Lynden, Washington, a small town near the Canadian border, where he had led his high school team to two straight state championships. At SPC, he established records in scoring and rebounding, and in 1965 was named an Associated Press second-team All-American.

The 1965 season brought still more excitement and joy to the campus and the entire city when the Falcons played their way into the NCAA Division II elite eight that spring. Although the University of North Dakota ousted them in the first round, the season put Seattle Pacific College on the map, and support continued to grow in Seattle for the local team.

The national quarterfinal tournament, held in Indiana, had occasioned a Habegger family reunion of sorts. The one person missing was Les's mother, Rosina, who had gone to Seattle to stay with Scott and Julie so that Anne could make the trip and cheer loyally for SPC. Although Les could never quite believe it, his siblings had always taken great pride in his accomplishments, and many of them traveled to Indianapolis to support his Falcons.

The clan came to cheer on another Habegger as well—Les's nephew Gary, one of the coach's superior recruits. Gary had transferred to Seattle Pacific after persuasive efforts by his uncle that had begun when he was in high school. He opted to go to Taylor University in Upland, Indiana, for his freshman year, but worked the following summer at the basketball camp on Whidbey Island.

Though Les may not have pressured him, Gary did recall being told, "I really would like to have you out here. I'd like to have you play out here." He talked it over with his father, Les's brother Eli, and then made the move to SPC for fall semester 1963. Gary played three successful years with the Falcons.

Games between Seattle Pacific and Seattle University, its much larger crosstown Jesuit rival, had grown into highly anticipated contests. Their meetings had become annual events in 1951, and though SPC had never won, Les, ever the optimist, said about the rivalry, "We never schedule a game I don't think we can win."

Both schools opened the 1965-66 season on December 1 when they met in the Seattle Center. A legacy of the city's Century 21 World's Fair in 1962, the Coliseum accommodated crowds larger than ten thousand. The Falcons played a good game and led well into the second half, maintaining a three- or four-point advantage until Seattle U tied things up with one minute and fourteen seconds remaining.

With ten seconds to go in the game, the score was still tied. On their final possession, SPC got the ball across the center line with two passes and into the hands of Gary Habegger. He took an eighteen-foot jump shot with one second on the clock and hit nothing but net. The next day, the headline on one of the local sports pages read, "Fearless Falcons Upset Chiefs, 85-83." Later, Les said, "To go on talking about it would be silly. But it sure is fun." As the victories began to pile up that year, it never ceased to be fun.

Their historic opener put the Falcons on the road to a 23-5 season; but when a loss to Pacific Lutheran knocked them from the unbeaten ranks, they fell from ninth to eleventh in the national small college rankings of United Press International. They made it into the NCAA postseason again, but placed second in the regional tournament, which prevented a return trip to the nationals.

The young men Les had assembled for that season's team

personified the scholar athlete. The team's grade point average was 3.0, which was more significant in the days before grade inflation. Four of the five starters were on the academic honors list—one history major and three math majors.

Those winning years were exhilarating. The team had a large and loyal faculty following; home games had become close to sellouts, and road games were usually broadcast on AM radio. Anne Habegger still made it to most home games. She found road games to be sheer agony, though.

"Oh my word, when they had away games and we could get it on the radio, I would pace the floor—I'd clean house, and listen to the game, and pace the floor, and pray, and cry, and clean." She recalled entertaining the players in the Habegger home above the campus. "We used to have a lot of parties, and wonderful times. I'd make big pans of lasagna. The guys loved it. And I was busy every minute. I still get hugs from some of them, you know."

Preparing to Win

With the graduation of several starters, Les predicted a downturn for the 1966-67 season. Although they struggled at times, the Falcons finished at 13-13—still not a losing record. But even as the victories had mounted in previous seasons, Les still could not take losses in stride. Anne said that after a victory, "Oh, he was jumping. I mean, he was exuberant. He was energized, and a lot of fun to be with. Otherwise, you wouldn't want to be near him if he lost. Following a loss, he was pretty morbid, and he wouldn't talk to anyone." Les and Anne frequently met friends for postgame parties, and she recalled that when SPC lost their friends would say, "Oh boy, we know what this night's going to be like."

Les could accept defeat at the hands of an all-around better team, but not when a loss was caused by mistakes that shouldn't have happened or lackadaisical play. He expected optimum preparation and maximum effort from his players as he pursued his coaching goal of preparing young men to reach their full potential. World War II had robbed him prematurely of his youth, but surviving it had left him with an iron will and the conviction, born of experience, that the human spirit enables a person to endure and overcome adversity beyond imagining. This certainty found its way into his practice schemes and fueled his reputation as a hard-nosed coach. "Conditioning to play is not fun," he acknowledged. "It is not easy; it is stark punishment." Although his approach was rooted in positive reinforcement, he brooked no nonsense and drove his players to exhaustion.

The annual basketball handbook he distributed to his players conveyed his priorities, his philosophy, and his determination in absolute terms: "The will to *prepare* must be greater than the will to win."

As for general conditioning and training, he asked, "Are you willing to pay the price to be a success? Are you willing to put out during every minute of practice? Games are won on the practice floor." He also said, "Let's have fun, but there's a difference between fun and 'horseplay.' It's much more fun to win than it is to lose. *Hustle* is our password."

Under the mental and spiritual heading, he asked, "Are you proud of yourself and your team? 'As a man thinketh in his heart, so is he.' Our actions result from our thoughts." He told them, "Playing ball at Seattle Pacific is a Christian service," and they should be willing to sacrifice to meet that challenge.

The handbook listed ten bedrock qualities he deemed *absolutely necessary for every good athlete*:

1. Are you coachable? Can you accept criticism?
2. Are you possessed with the spirit of competition that fires an intense desire to win?

3. Are you willing to practice? Will you work every day with the same zeal, speed, and determination you use in a game?

4. Are you willing to make sacrifices? Will you deny yourself in order to remain in tip-top condition (which has its rewards)?

5. Do you have an ardent desire to improve?

6. Do you have the ability to think under fire?

7. Are you willing to be impersonal toward your opponents? (Les believed that the minute a player made it personal, he ceased to play basketball as a team member.)

8. Do you believe in your school, your team, your coach?

9. Are you willing to study just as hard as you did before you came out for basketball? The athletic tail must never wag the academic dog.

10. Will you strive daily to improve your muscular coordination and speed? (Les never strayed from physical conditioning.) Speed and coordination are necessary ingredients for winning.

The daily practice sessions that found his players in Royal Brougham Pavilion every afternoon by about 2:30, revolved around rules implied in the ten bedrock qualities. Those practices were well-planned, well-organized, and goal oriented.

Most SPC players would probably agree that Les was fair, but they would also agree that he was a taskmaster. They were expected to train during summer vacations and be fit to run a mile in a given time before school started. Gary Habegger gave an example of Les's enforcement of preseason conditioning.

Before the season started in the fall, we would have training, and we would run the sand hills over at Queen Anne Bowl, a nearby park. The guards had to run a mile in . . . five minutes thirty seconds—something like that . . . So we came back in the fall of '65, and we were going to run the distances; but after we had run a half mile, he blew his whistle and said, "Stop, stop! Everybody stop. I forgot to start the stopwatch! So line up again, and we're going to run the mile, and you still need to make your time." Not many of us made our times the second time around, because we'd already run a half mile. As a result, we had sand hills to run, because we hadn't made our times. Most of us were very upset about that. We always thought he really had started the stopwatch—that it was deliberate on his part. He stopped us halfway through to start us over again.

Given Les's conviction that a person can endure more than one thinks, they may have been right.

Les admitted to being a taskmaster, but it was always within the context of his desire "to make men out of young kids." For Les, this included discipline, organization, and working hard. "We were created in the image of God, and it's our responsibility to act accordingly. We were engineered for success. We are to be successful. We're here to win, because that's our duty. That's our responsibility as people. So I pushed winning, and I emphasized that winning may not be the most important thing, but preparing to win is. I emphasized that you are to *think*, *prepare*, and *work* to win. If winning doesn't come, so be it; but proper *preparation* to win is the most important thing."

Preparing to win became his hallmark. His practices began long before the players arrived, when he could be found in his office poring over notes from the previous day to find weaknesses they needed to work on. "He was first and foremost a teacher from the 'whole/part/ whole' school, and never lost sight of the whole picture." He drilled repetitiously on component parts, such as setting a proper screen, before putting it all together. He knew these drills did not please his players, who complained about never getting to scrimmage. But he credited his coaching success to "repetition, repetition, repetition" and "practicing as nearly perfect as possible."

He did not consider punishment or sarcasm helpful motivational tools. He said, "You don't punish, you encourage. It should be, 'This is the way you do it,' not, 'You lousy rebounder, you don't rebound worth a—'" Even so, as he recalled, when things did not go right, "I'd get mad and I'd yell, 'Get on the end line!'" This command signaled the beginning of "line sprints"—seemingly endless sprinting from baseline to free throw line and back.

Jim Ballard recalled that disciplinary action typically followed lack of effort. "If he thought we were dogging it, he would do something physically to get our attention. And it became real clear early on that if you didn't want to run line drills, you worked hard." It was also clear that the whole team paid for anyone's lack of effort. "So you'd get on the other teammate in the locker room and say, 'Hey, quit dogging it. I don't want to run line drills at the end of practice.'"

More than one session ended with Les saying, "Okay, you're going to run. Yeah, we're through with practice, but you're going to run for fifteen more minutes." In addition to line sprints, they ran distances.

Decades later, Les would ask, "Was that right? I don't know." He does know that some former players now appreciate his principles. "But at the time, they hated me."

Falcon team boosters continued to drive the team to away games, but by the late 1960s there were other options as well. John Glancy, who played from 1966 through 1970 remembered, "We took a bus to Spokane once; took a train to Spokane once; and, of course, if it were somewhat farther than that, we would fly." Trains and planes took them to games in Montana and California. Gary Habegger had one unforgettable trip to California in his senior year that involved plane, automobile, and his Uncle Les's reaction to losing.

The team had flown to Fresno that spring for the regional tournament, and Del Kreider, a longtime backer of Falcon sports, had driven down to watch the games. When they lost the final game—which meant they would not be going back to Evansville for the national tournament—Les was not happy. When it came time to return home, they were short one plane ticket, so Les said to Gary, "You're not going to fly back. You're going to ride in the car with Del Kreider and me."

Gary really did not want to do that. "I knew he took it very hard and was somewhat upset with the way we played during the game. And then I had to ride all the way back to Seattle with him in the car." The drive took about eighteen hours then, but it seemed even longer to Gary. He said, "We drove it straight through, and Del and Les traded off driving. I was just in the back seat, and there was very little conversation the whole way home."

Les despised losing. He expected superior effort from his players, and he drove them hard to get it. He attributed his work ethic to a combination of things—his Amish heritage, army service, World War II, competition, coaching, a positive outlook, and his Christian beliefs. "That's who I am," he said.

Life in the Habegger Household

Children of a prominent coach lead unique lives. It is not easy to share your father with the public. He is in demand as a speaker in the community; he often works late into the night in his office; he is frequently away from home on road trips and may miss important milestones such as birthdays. As one coach's daughter put it, "You have to come to terms with who your parent is, and accept that he can't be all things."

Decades later, Les's daughter, Julie, said, "I don't ever remember a time of Dad not being a winning coach. . . . Those early years were good years, but Scott and I would often end up staying at home with sitters while our parents attended various functions." On Sunday, however, the whole family could be found in church school and worship services at Seattle's University Presbyterian Church.

Traces of World War II hovered over the Habegger household decades after the war. Julie recalled that the war was always there; though fading, it never left. "When I was younger—he would have been out of the war for twenty some years, but it was still pretty fresh. I would wake him up and he would jump and have this look—not quite sure where he was, but definitely on the defensive." The whole family saw that. They would ask questions, but he never talked about the war. He would just change the subject.

He did work his army experience into parenting on a lighter note, however. Julie laughed as she recounted one of his better motivational techniques. "When we were little kids, we played 'inspection,' one of his games to get us to clean up our rooms. My brother and I were in competition; we were privates and had to make our beds and clean up our rooms, and we would stand by our beds like we were soldiers. It was humorous, but as kids we took it very seriously. This had been his experience, so he invented this game to get us to clean our rooms. . . . It was a game to him, he'd walk around and make sure everything was in order, and then he'd say 'At ease,' salute, and leave." Les would then return, announce who had the cleanest room, and give the victor a trinket or toy.

Julie remembered that her dad traveled a lot, but even Les's being away from home had an upside. "We learned early to greet him at the door and ask what he had brought. He always brought us something." Scott and Julie had a bit of star power of their own on the close-knit Seattle Pacific campus. Their friends were all faculty children and their dad was The Coach. They went to most home games and had the run of the pavilion. At the same time, they felt a certain pressure as public figures. Although Les did not make an issue of it or pressure them to be good, Julie always felt they had an image to protect.

Sons of popular and successful coaches are often subjected to unreasonable community expectation that they will follow in their fathers' footsteps. When Scott Habegger was six years old, during the magical 1965-66 season, *The Falcon* ran an article that revealed how the coach's son felt about things. The article, titled "A Coach's Wife and Mid-winter Madness," reported that Scott had told his dad he wanted to be a basketball player, but added that he had confided to his mother, "I just tell Daddy I'm going to be a basketball player to make him happy, but I'm really going to be a fireman." Les may or may not have pressured Scott, and Scott did play, but he had other interests.

Decades later, thinking back to the summers when his son worked at the basketball camp, Les said, "I think I might have 'shell-shocked' Scott" with overexposure to motivational principles and an emphasis on winning. He ruefully recalled Scott telling him one day at the camp, after a staff game that his team lost, "Dad, you don't know what it's like to be your son. People expect me to be as good as you." Scott later turned to rodeo and bull riding; he had found something his dad could not do. From early childhood, he had loved animals. His room was home to hamsters, lizards, and other small critters. His experience working with large rodeo animals may have been what led him to a successful career as an equine veterinarian.

The basketball camp on Whidbey Island was the Habegger family summer home, and Les was always there with them. They rented a faculty house at Camp Casey, and those summer memories are among the family's strongest and fondest. The children had the run of the whole area, and their parents felt no uneasiness about letting them go off on their own. Their only worries concerned safety around such natural hazards as the beach's undertow. As Les recalled, "Scott was two years old when we started that camp, and I hear him now tell other people what a great summer home he had. He was up there every day, every summer."

Looking back decades later, Julie too had fond memories. "It was a good, safe, wholesome environment. The whole family was there, school was out—all the pressure was gone. It was just an idyllic area. We would say good-bye in the morning, and at that time nobody said there could be strange people out there and you had to be careful. We would just take off, play on the beach, build forts, go up to the old army fort, come in and eat lunch and go out again—it was just all-day activity."

Children of the other coaches who joined the camp staff were there, so they never lacked for playmates. Evenings found the Habegger family all together, tired and happy. Julie said, "I'll never forget that good worn-out feeling from playing all day, . . . and the fire in the fireplace, a driftwood fire, and the smell, . . . and we would make popcorn on the stove. The house just smelled like driftwood and the ocean air, so it was magical that way—the atmosphere—it just was wonderful for kids."

Les recalled those times with his children at the camp when they were very young. Scott was a ball boy, and Les later put him to work in the kitchen, as well. "It was a great experience for him," he said. It indeed seemed idyllic, and Les thought it was "marvelous" for the whole family.

BEYOND THE X'S AND O'S

When the family returned to Seattle at the end of those summers, Les went back to the task of building his Seattle Pacific teams. By the fall of 1967, he was eligible for a sabbatical leave; but coming off a 13-13 season, he declined the opportunity and accepted President Demaray's contract offer of $11,000, with the rank of associate professor and director of athletics for 1967-68. By then, too, he had received more than a few overtures from other schools, so the president's offer letter ended firmly with, "By all means, we expect you and want you to continue your coaching position with us."

Knowing how their coach responded to losses and frustration, the six holdover players from the 1966-67 team may or may not have welcomed the news that he was not going on leave. He continued to expect maximum effort and no less than total dedication from his players. Complaints had begun to arise on the campus that Les might have recruited some less-than-committed Christians to play for him; but he held fast to his own practices and beliefs, such as winning being an obligation for athletes created in God's image. One player from the late 1960s recalled thinking, "A lot of the guys on the team did not have a close relationship with God," but even though Les didn't push it all the time, they knew it was important to him.

Bill Yeager epitomized a different type of player for SPC, and his career exemplified the influence of Les Habegger in the lives of his players. After playing two years at Everett Community College, in 1965 Yeager was widely recruited and entertained by virtually every coach in the Pacific Northwest. He recalled, "Les Habegger called and said, 'I'd like to have you come to Seattle Pacific,' and that was it. That's all there was to it. There was no meeting, there was no nothing. It's a Christian school, and my folks thought that was really a bad move. I called him back two days later and said, 'I'm on my way.' There was absolutely no reason for me to show up at Seattle Pacific College, and attend chapel, and do all that stuff."

Yeager showed up, but he said that after being there for about two months, "I was absolutely devastated that I had made that choice. I wanted out of there so bad, I couldn't even see straight; but I stayed. I don't know why I stayed, either." Yeager stayed on through the 1967-68 season, and was a big factor in SPC's turnaround from 13-13 to 16-9. He was named a Small College All-American that year, and later played professionally for a team in Lyon, France.

As for his decision to attend Seattle Pacific, Yeager said, "I came to strongly believe there was some kind of divine intervention there, at a time when I had no idea what divine intervention was." He feels now that Les Habegger was the key. "You know, there was something about him the very first time I met him, and I was too young to put my finger on it; but for whatever reason, I think I had a lot of confidence and a lot of faith in him, and it had nothing to do with his record." Along with many other former players, Yeager cited lessons learned that went far beyond the X's and O's, including focus, preparation, visualization. Some, he said, "I still use to this day on a daily basis. For some reason, that guy was supposed to be in my life at that time, and Lord only knows where I would have been without him, or where I would have ended up if I would have left after two months, like I wanted to."

WINDS OF CHANGE

Dr. Demaray, with whom Les had enjoyed an amicable relationship, retired in the spring of 1968. Wesley Lingren, professor of chemistry and longtime member of the Faculty Athletic Committee, characterized Demaray's approach to athletics as *relaxed*. "He just turned it over, to do what you want." Demaray's successor, David L. McKenna, came that fall from Spring Arbor College in Michigan. Lingren saw a contrast in the two presidents' philosophies, with McKenna's being that "the president controls athletics." Seattle Pacific's department of athletics would continue to produce winners as the dynamics of governance underwent some modification.

Dr. McKenna arrived at a time of challenges on the campus and of social upheaval in Seattle. The civil rights movement came slowly to the Pacific Northwest, but by the late 1960s, Seattle's university campuses had begun to experience racial controversy. Cultural revolution and campus social rebellion moved quickly up the coast from San Francisco and Berkeley, and the district around the University of Washington became the countercultural center of the city. The more sheltered Seattle Pacific campus experienced aftershocks from those earthquakes, and the faculty sought ways to deal with them in accord with the commitments of a Christian college.

Seattle Pacific had a predominantly white, Protestant student body, but Les's teams of that era included some African-American players. In recruiting, Les always explained the nature of the college to potential Falcons, so that they were aware, for example, that they had to take a course in religion and attend daily chapel. Such conditions and requirements affected the team's racial makeup. Les also said that SPC's low minority enrollment had a negative impact on recruiting, and many black players chose not to attend Seattle Pacific.

The matter of Les's experience with minority players became an issue in 1971. A coaching vacancy opened up at the University of Washington when Tex Winter left the college ranks for the NBA. Joe Kearney, UW's athletic director, was a Seattle Pacific graduate and Les's good friend. Kearney asked Les if he was interested in the job and invited him to his home to discuss things. They met late one week, and the following Sunday, the front page of the Seattle *Post-Intelligencer* carried a photo of Les and proclaimed that he was to be named the Huskies' head coach.

The proverbial feathers soon hit the fan. There had been an ugly, ongoing controversy over the treatment of African-American players in the UW football program; the Black Student Union had gained considerable influence, and now weighed in against the prospect of Les Habegger becoming the basketball coach. Their main objection was that his coaching experience at Seattle Pacific was in a small school where he had little or no involvement with African-American students; hence, they said, he was unqualified. Kearney then, of necessity, formed a selection committee and asked Les to formally apply. Les recalled telling him, "Joe, we're friends, but you know as well as I do I'm not going to get the job, because they've already said they don't want me." He withdrew his name from further consideration.

Les recalled another instance in which his hopes of coaching at a Division I school suffered a reversal. When coach Paul Valenti left Oregon State, the OSU athletic director invited Les to Corvallis for an interview. He accepted the invitation, and later said, "I had a great time down there—a great interview, a lot of fun. I had been stationed in Oregon, right outside of Corvallis, during the war."

He definitely was in the running for the job. However, the possibility was raised that Seattle Pacific's trustees might take the school into Division I for basketball. That possibility and the college's commitment to Christian principles weighed heavily in Les's decision to withdraw his name from consideration at Oregon State. He later revealed a trace of his old feeling of unworthiness, when he said, "Obviously I wouldn't have gotten it anyway." The Beavers ultimately hired Ralph Miller, who built Oregon State into a national Division I basketball power over the next nineteen years.

In his inaugural address in October 1968, President McKenna had emphasized change, saying, "Seattle Pacific College has no option other than to change." He went on to restructure departments and programs, and led the school to university status. As head basketball coach and athletic director, Les Habegger dealt with considerable change. Even as he confronted such challenges as Title IX and the growth of women's sports, he continued to mold strong and tenacious players into what had become his and Seattle Pacific's hallmark: competitive, winning teams.

CHAPTER TEN

SUCCESS AND MORE CHANGE

Over the next several years, Seattle Pacific continued to compile winning records in Brougham Pavilion and on the road. They finished the 1967-68 season with sixteen wins against nine losses, and narrowly missed another trip to the NCAA tournament with a loss to Portland State in the next to last regular season game. Their first season in the David McKenna era ended at 16-10.

President McKenna soon set change in motion, took a more direct control of athletics, and played a larger role in setting priorities. Early changes in the order of governance had the athletic director now reporting to the vice president, and eventually to the dean of academic affairs. Campus politics are a wondrous thing, and under the new administration, Les could no longer go to his backers and friends on the board of trustees for the sort of direct support he had enjoyed under President Demaray. Some jurisdictional friction was all but inevitable. Nevertheless, in the small, close-knit Seattle Pacific community, the McKenna and Habegger families became good friends. They made the rounds socially together, and in a sense personified the college to the public.

President McKenna inherited a severe financial crisis. In his first year in Seattle, he imposed across-the-board budget cuts of 33 percent, which forced all departments and programs to retrench. At one point during the budget crisis, Les had to appeal to his equipment suppliers to extend credit for such necessities as shoes and uniforms for the basketball team. As athletic director, Les faced the painful job of overseeing deep cuts in athletics. The tennis and baseball programs were immediately cut, and wrestling soon followed.

By this time, Ken Foreman had returned to coaching and had built the Seattle Pacific track program into one of national acclaim. His protégée, Doris Brown, had run the 800 meters in 2:03.9 at the Olympic Games in Mexico City. Les's basketball team and Foreman's women's track team kept SPC in the sports spotlight. Scholarship money had always been limited, and the budget restrictions forced a revision of priorities. Professor Lingren said that what emerged was the idea of "selective excellence." "We focused most of our scholarship money, all of it, in fact, on those two sports, the ones we thought would get us the best mileage in the city, and with our coaches."

BUILDING CHARACTER ON THE COURT

In 1969, Les invested much of the basketball program's share of scholarship money in only the second full-ride offer he'd ever made. When Lingren returned from a chemistry conference in Denver with a sports page from the *Denver Post* listing its all-city players, Les wrote to every one of them. Jim Ballard, whose high school team had won the state championship, was the only one who responded.

Ballard later remembered being recruited "sight unseen," and thinking, "Wow. Being eighteen, I wanted to get as far away from my parents as I could, so the whole idea of going to the Northwest was really appealing. So this just seemed like a good fit." He also remembered meeting Les at his first practice. "I found it pretty intimidating, until I realized most of the guys that were there were just as scared as I was." He began to hear what a demanding, tough coach Les was, and soon had some stories of his own to add to the lore.

Ballard echoed others in saying that Les was strict and exacting; that he expected complete preparation and "a certain level of conditioning, both mentally and physically," which many people saw as being "a little too much." Ballard thought so, too, but now he says, "It was an integral part of teaching us that we are capable of going beyond our limits—both physical and mental."

Ballard recalled a rather extreme example of Les's teaching style (vividly remembered by others as well), which followed a lackadaisical road loss to Central Washington State College in Ellensburg.

After driving the hundred miles back to Seattle and arriving on the SPC campus at 2:00 a.m., everyone was exhausted. It had been a humiliating loss.

"Coach was really upset," Ballard recalled. "I happened to be riding in his car, and it was quiet the whole way back. We got back, and he unloaded everything and got our equipment out, and then he said, 'Go suit up.' We all looked at him like, 'What?' And he said, 'Go suit up. I want you on the floor in fifteen minutes.' And so we actually suited up and ran drills at two o'clock in the morning. . . . He was very passionate about planning, preparation, and execution, and when we didn't accomplish that, there were typically consequences. . . . As much as I didn't like those consequences at the time, I truly, truly appreciate them now."

Jim Ballard played four seasons for Seattle Pacific and was named to the All-America team three times. His freshman fears and intimidation had begun to fade, he said, when he realized that Les "not only cared about me as a basketball player, he also cared about me as a person—and I saw that demonstrated toward the other guys as well, to varying degrees. He had an amazing ability to recognize the character and personalities of the players, and he could alter his approach to get the maximum effort and performance out of us. His approach ranged from quiet, positive reinforcement to screaming and hollering and yelling, which, for some guys got them up off their butts and got them going."

Three decades later, and by then a successful businessman, Ballard confirmed that Les had more than achieved his goal of influencing the lives of Christian athletes. "One thing I really appreciated about Habegger was his strong belief in God, including his belief in the saving grace of Jesus Christ upon the cross. That was probably more important to me than I realized at the time—to go to a Christian college and have a Christian coach; and yeah, that faith in God was somewhat stabilizing."

When Don DeHart graduated from high school, he was not specifically seeking a Christian college; but he recalled being scouted by Les's assistant coach, Loren Miller. Friends in DeHart's home church in Santa Clara, California, were relatives of Roy Glancy, a Queen Anne resident and one of the Falcons' strongest supporters. So, in February of 1970, during his senior year at Cupertino High, DeHart visited the SPC campus. He met Les and saw the team in action, liked the style of play and approach to the game, and thought he could learn a lot. After accepting Les's offer to come to SPC, DeHart thrived in the hard-driving system, and was another who learned a lot more from Les than X's and O's. DeHart succeeded Jim Ballard as team captain for the 1973-74 season, and said it was during Les's traditional weekly lunches with his captains that he absorbed the coach's bedrock philosophy: "how you live life—work, friendship, faith."

During DeHart's sophomore year, his on-court actions in a playoff game in Pueblo, Colorado, brought a rare courtside outburst from Les, who charged that his team had been "homered." In the finals of the 1972 divisional regional tournament, Seattle Pacific lost to Southern Colorado State, 86-83. The game was played on Southern Colorado's home court and officiated by referees chosen by their coach. The game was widely reported, and Les was quoted as shouting for all to hear at the end of the game, "We got jobbed, and everybody in this place knows it!"

Several calls had gone against the Falcons throughout the game, but they still led most of the way, and clearly out-played Southern Colorado until the incident that fueled Les's outrage. John Garrett, a columnist from Riverside, California, described the scene: "Don DeHart scooped up a loose ball and Southern Colorado's Dan England, diving for the ball and missing, slammed into him." After words were exchanged, "DeHart threw the ball at England, [who] came up swinging and had to be restrained by the officials." When order was restored, DeHart received a flagrant foul and was ejected from the game. England was not penalized and sank two free throws before Southern Colorado was awarded the ball out of bounds—all of which turned the game around at that point.

A bit later, and a bit calmer, Les would say, "My kid was wrong; he was stupid for doing that. But you don't throw a guy out of a game for throwing the ball. . . . I'll argue with them until sundown." Still later, and much calmer, he reflected on his own role in the incident: "I have always felt I was man enough to take defeat when it came, rather than charge the referees for the loss. But I honestly and sincerely felt that SCS didn't beat us because they were a better team; that there were some other factors. If that classifies me as a bad sport or a guy who doesn't take his losses, I guess that's what it is."

John Garrett pinpointed another thing that bothered Les the most: "What happened to Seattle Pacific would never have been allowed to happen to [a Division I] team, because of the glare of national publicity."

By the autumn of 1972, Les and his players had put the controversy and fracas in Pueblo behind them, finishing the season at 16-9. Don DeHart later said that Les always admonished them "not to leave anything on the floor. He didn't want you to become accustomed to or enjoy losing." With DeHart as captain, the team went on to compile a 15-11 record in 1974.

Les said he was fortunate to have such high-caliber assistant coaches during his years at Seattle Pacific. His early assistants included Bernie Buck, Dick Kamm, Chuck Alm, and longtime assistant Roland Halle, a University of Washington graduate, who had played on the all-Navy team involved in tryouts for the Melbourne Olympics in 1956. Daniel Stautz joined the staff as freshman coach in 1965. A three-year letterman at Seattle University, Stautz had graduated from Bremerton High School, the alma mater of Dave Wortman, a mainstay SPC player and honorable mention all-American in 1962. Loren Miller had been a four-year letterman at Sterling College in Kansas, and Keith Swagerty had played professional basketball in the old ABA before Les hired him as a Seattle Pacific assistant in the early 1970s.

From time to time, Les also relied on his former players to help with coaching. Dave Wortman and his brother Gary both returned as assistants for a time, as did Howard Heppner. As John Glancy recalled, "Dave Wortman is one that Les used quite a bit. Occasionally, he'd bring in others who might be in the area, and they were very helpful, I'm sure, to Les." In Les's whole-part-whole teaching approach, his assistants would often work with small groups on specialized training.

"In a typical practice session," John Glancy recalled, "Les would break down the practice into different components—so we would work on a segment of the offense, or a segment of the defense. Then we'd come together, usually at the end of practice, to run the plays as a unit; and we'd ultimately have a scrimmage, to try and put all the stuff together."

TITLE IX TIGHTROPE

Though Les supported all of SPC's sports across the board, women's as well as men's, he did not greet the 1972 advent of Title IX with unbounded joy. As athletic director, he was obligated to implement equal programs and facilities for men and women. He laughed when he later recalled his immediate declaration: "No way am I going to let women into the training room!"

Aside from his personal reservations, he was faced with the challenge of spreading the always scarce funds even thinner. Professor Lingren said, "Title IX forced us into playing women's sports on an equal basis with men, and Les was grumpy about it because it took money away." Seattle Pacific might have had a slight advantage, though, because Ken Foreman's potent women's track program had put the school on the national map for women's sports. Also, as Les said, "SPC had women's basketball way back when it was a half-court game," but until Title IX, they'd had no women's intercollegiate program.

One serendipitous thing that eased the Title IX pressure was the 1972 purchase of property from a lumber company along West Nickerson Way, the major arterial bordering the campus on the north. In addition to a broad expanse, fittingly named Wallace Field in honor of Dr. Marvin Wallace, the longtime benefactor of Falcon athletics, the tract included a building adjacent to Brougham Pavilion that was converted into the women's gym and an indoor track facility.

Les had added a number of sports during his tenure as athletic director, including both men's and women's crew, soccer, wrestling, tennis, and women's gymnastics; but during the budget crunch he had been forced to cut tennis, baseball, and wrestling. He knew that the cuts weren't popular. The biggest bone of contention was basketball's allocation from the athletic budget, which other coaches complained about. Men's basketball remained at the top of Les's priority list, and he continued to pursue his goals and to demand the best from his players. Les remained committed to motivating Christian athletes; but by this time, some on the campus thought that not all the players he recruited bought wholeheartedly into the Habegger message, and not all were faith-driven.

CRITICISM AND CONTROVERSY

Change was in the wind as the college moved toward university status. Professor Lingren, from his position on the faculty athletic committee, saw that Les and President McKenna remained close friends off campus, "But professionally, they had a real tangle over the idea of who was running athletics." If *The Falcon*, the student newspaper, mirrored opinion, a major shift had occurred in the attitude on campus toward athletics. Editorials critical of athletic priorities began to appear during the 1973-74 basketball season.

Oddly enough, the decision to drop junior varsity basketball brought the paper's first blast. The lead editorial on October 12 claimed to be "a plea for the athletic department to come to their senses." It charged that Les saw the JV as "merely a farm club for the varsity, [and he] figures that the few [varsity prospects] can practice with the varsity, removing the need for a JV." The article also noted that President McKenna was "not aware of the pending decision."

Despite the controversy, with six veteran players returning, Les was optimistic as the season opened. On November 2, *The Falcon* hinted at discord among the players, even as it reported that the team was excited about the season. "Any incidents of the past, such as grumblings about Habegger, are forgotten now, and there is a great deal of team unity."

The Falcon heralded the season opener on November 30 with a long feature titled, "It's Time for the Money Sport Again," which emphasized that the team was "coming off a record year at the box office." Quoting Les as saying he was tired, the article said, "That's understandable when you consider his concern. Habegger faces a dilemma more far-reaching than courtside. . . . Add to [the loss of two big men] an intra-person conflict over basketball's significance on campus, and you have a problem. . . . [The] question is whether basketball serves a real purpose on campus. Does support of the team depend on a won-loss record, or an attitude of sincere effort from its players?"

The rest of the article included a somewhat mangled version of Les's coaching philosophy. Saying that if team support turned on effort, Falcon fans had something to cheer about. After describing a player who "turns low points into high ones by diving after a loose ball, or shouting encouragement to teammates," the writer concluded by saying, "This kind of hustle jibes well with Habegger's philosophy of taking chances. The coach asserts that one has to 'risk everything' in life before he will feel satisfied. Winning is not the result, but the effort."

Although Seattle Pacific did not make it to the postseason, they finished the year with a record of 15-11. Les's basketball program continued to receive scrutiny in the *The Falcon*'s sports columns, and criticism that had not appeared in earlier years. One of the most pointed articles appeared on April 4, 1974, under the heading, "Big Money Sports Shouldn't Suffocate Other Athletics." Again calling basketball "the money sport," the sportswriter allowed that the players were "worth their budget." Nevertheless, he asked, "is the purpose of the athletic department to have one showcase sport which will get the major portion of the cake and at the same time bring in more money for all sports, or is the purpose to provide a comprehensive program with equal funding for all, regardless of sex and the sport? . . . Is our program one of professionalism, where all we are concerned about is winning, or should it be geared to providing a chance for as many as possible to participate equally in the luxuries that go with each sport?"

One month later, the front page of *The Falcon* bore a photo of Les under the headline, "Coach Habegger To Be Gone Next Year." The sports information director had declined to comment, but some players said that Les had told them he would take a sabbatical leave to observe the athletic and basketball programs at several universities, possibly including UCLA, USC and Indiana. Les had indicated to them that he would be "contemplating his future plans," with the possible option of returning as just the athletic director or continuing as head basketball coach and athletic director. Implied in what he said was the possibility of not returning at all. The student reporter added, "The position and future of the athletic director has been much discussed the last few years."

Decades later, Les mused, "Toward the end of my career at Seattle Pacific, I think I had worn out my welcome. I think the truth of it is that the president wanted me to leave." In 1974, President McKenna had taken note of the fact that it had been eighteen years since Les had arrived on campus, and told him, "You need a sabbatical. You haven't had [one]. . . . You need to go on sabbatical."

SOUTHLAND SABBATICAL

By this time, Les had begun to ponder his future. He asked himself, "What do I do? What direction do I take? Am I doing the right thing?" He made a chance phone call to John Wooden, whose UCLA teams had won ten Division I national titles. "I did not personally know John Wooden," he said, "but I had seen him at clinics, and at games and so on. So, I called John, told him who I was, and said, 'Could I spend a year watching your program?'" The result was a gracious invitation from the legendary coach for Les to go down to Westwood and observe. Les spent a rewarding and enjoyable sabbatical leave in southern California.

His sister Martha and her husband had moved to San Diego in 1958, and she secured a house there for Les and Anne to rent. Scott and Julie were now in middle school and Anne had resumed her teaching career, but the school district granted her a leave for the year, with the understanding that she would use the time in part earn additional credits. So, as Les was driving up to the UCLA campus, and the kids were at school, Anne enrolled at San Diego State College. She recalled, "I had to take credits towards a master's. So I took a full load. I think I had seventeen hours—it was a big load." Always before, she had worked while going to school, but this time, "I didn't have to work," so she did well and enjoyed the graduate program.

Les, for his part, spent much of his sabbatical leave with fellow Hoosier, John Wooden, the Wizard of Westwood, in what would be the last year of Wooden's incredible coaching career. Les said, "I would drive up I-405 to Los Angeles each morning, and spend my time at UCLA with John Wooden—and I had a marvelous year with him. He was an amazing man. He didn't know me, but he gave me time, whatever I wanted. I'd sit in his office and pick his brain about basketball; we'd go to lunch together; I'd go to his practices; and I was able to see what his practices were like."

Les was amazed at how Wooden had shared himself with him, and he came to view the coach as "without a doubt, the Master Motivator." He found that they both stressed simplicity, fundamentals, and visualization; and he found confirmation of his own approach to coaching and everything he thought about the right and wrong way to deal with players. In planning his sabbatical, he had decided to go straight to the top and learn how "the best coach in the business" operated. He was more than gratified to discover that his own approach was not far from what Coach Wooden was doing at UCLA.

A Changing of the Guard

All good things must come to an end, and after his "fabulous year with John," Les returned home to find that the landscape had changed at Seattle Pacific while he was away. President McKenna and several influential boosters had been well pleased with the performance of Les's assistant, Keith Swagerty, who had coached the team during Les's sabbatical. Ultimately, the decision was made to retain Swagerty as head coach.

Les had returned to Seattle refreshed by a change of scene and energized by his association with John Wooden and the rapport they had established. But he came back to a campus in the midst of reorganization. President McKenna had created schools of various disciplines, and he now asked Les to head the School of Physical Education and Athletics. This gave Les greater academic responsibility, and he recalled holding the position reluctantly during that first year back. He served on the academic council with the directors of other schools, and attended faculty meetings. "This was all good, and fairly satisfying," he said, "but I missed coaching." Following the chain of command, he went to the dean, and said, "I don't want this directorship. I'm a basketball coach. I want my job back." The dean was sympathetic, but the decision was not his to make.

When President McKenna did not reinstate him as Seattle Pacific's basketball coach, Les quit and left the school in the summer of 1976. During his tenure at Seattle Pacific, his salary had grown from the $3900 that had drawn him from Minneapolis in 1956 to $20,000 twenty years later. In recognition of his years of service, the board of trustees commended Les in a letter, and presented him with a $5000 stipend, as their "best evidence of appreciation for the work you did in raising athletics to prominence at SPC."

During his two decades on the SPC campus, Les had become widely known in the Seattle area as a talented and resourceful motivational speaker. When he found himself in a "coaching wilderness," he took advantage of his speaking ability and, in the summer of 1976, joined a motivational enterprise known as the Learning Institute. The focus of the business was in the field of education, and Les held seminars for teachers and coaches, dealing with such things as building teenage self-esteem. Later, he expanded into working with business groups, presenting seminars on motivation and team-building for groups as diverse as automobile dealers and certified public accountants. He continued to be in demand as a speaker even after he returned to coaching basketball.

CHAPTER ELEVEN

THE NBA COMES TO
THE PACIFIC NORTHWEST

In the twenty years since Les and Anne Habegger had arrived at Seattle Pacific College, both the school and the city had grown and changed. When Seattle's business and civic leadership launched a drive to stage Century 21, the 1962 World Exposition, the entire population supported it. That World's Fair shook Seattle from its lingering provincialism and moved it beyond its regional focus. Among the tangible legacies of Century 21 was a first-class sports arena that enabled Seattle to enter the world of professional basketball. By 1980, the city boasted an NBA championship, a triumph in which Les played a crucial role.

In 1966, the NBA awarded an expansion franchise to California businessman Sam Schulman and his partners, for a team that would play at the Seattle Center Coliseum in the shadow of the Space Needle. Schulman became the active partner and head of team operations. A public contest to name the new team brought more than 25,000 entries. Many reflected the city's history, with suggestions ranging from its Native American roots to the jet age. Fortunately, such possibilities as the Seattle Loggers and the Seattle Stevedores did not make the cut. Instead, with a nod to the local aerospace industry, the region's largest employer, and an optimistic look to the future, the team became the Seattle Supersonics.

The team soon became known simply as the Sonics. Dropping the "Super" may or may not have been a byproduct of the expansion team's first season, in which they drew an average of only 6,524 per game to the Coliseum and ended with a 23-59 won/loss record. That 1967-68 team had some stellar players, including All-Star guard Walt Hazzard, well known in Seattle for the years he played for John Wooden at UCLA. During the off-season, the Sonics traded Hazzard to Atlanta for another All-Star, Lenny Wilkens; and at the end of the second season, which produced thirty wins, Wilkens was named head coach.

Sam Schulman made a bold move against the rival American Basketball Association when he signed its MVP, Spencer Haywood, for the 1971-72 season. This provoked the ABA to mount a long legal battle that went all the way to the U.S. Supreme Court, but it proved worth the fight when the team and its fans enjoyed their first winning season. The euphoria was short lived, however, when the popular Wilkens was sent to Cleveland the next year, in a trade that upset the fans and contributed to a 26-56 season record. Bill Russell, the Boston Celtic great, took over the coaching reins for the 1973-74 season, and in his second year, the team made its first playoff appearance.

THE SONICS AND SPC

Soon after the arrival of the Sonics, a link was forged between the team and Seattle Pacific College. Royal Brougham Pavilion lay just over Queen Anne Hill from the Coliseum in Seattle Center. Les, who was still SPC's athletic director at the time, recalled, "The Sonics came to me and said, 'Could we use your floor for our practices?' So

I made a deal—and rather than pay rent for the building, they gave me tickets for the games. In those days, the Sonics weren't drawing much, so we got front row seats on the floor," which he shared with others across the campus.

When the financial situation that hamstrung the SPC athletic budget forced Les to cut the wrestling program, it worked to the Sonics' advantage. Coach Frank Furtado had built a tremendous wrestling program in addition to teaching in the physical education department. When the Sonics moved into Brougham Pavilion to practice, Les asked Furtado if he was interested in making some extra money by maintaining the locker room and handling the uniform laundry for the Sonics. Not long after Bill Russell came on board as the Sonics' coach, "he took a liking to Frank, and asked him to replace the team's departing trainer." Furtado, who had taught athletic conditioning at SPC, accepted this new challenge. As Les recalled, "He trained on the job; he went to some clinics, and he became a fabulous trainer."

Sarah Furtado, Frank's wife, had been Les's secretary in the Seattle Pacific athletic office. In 1970, she assumed a secretarial role with the Sonics organization. When the Sonics needed a seasoned talent scout, not long after Les left SPC in 1976, Sarah suggested they hire her former boss.

So, while continuing to teach motivational courses through the Learning Institute, Les also scouted local college games for the Sonics. He knew both Bill Russell and his assistant, Bob Hopkins, and when Hopkins became head coach when Russell left in the spring of 1977, he invited Les to become his assistant coach.

Les had a lot of misgivings about going into the pro game. In coaching college players, with his whole-part-whole teaching foundation, he had insisted on fundamentals. In his close-range observations of the pro game, he had concluded, "It was not really basketball the way I wanted to teach it. I wanted to coach players, and my impression of the NBA had been that you just throw out the ball." On the other hand, he knew he wanted to get back into coaching. He decided, "I'll give it a shot."

TOUGH TIMES AND A TURNAROUND

The late 1970s were not a promising time in Sonics history for Les to start his NBA coaching career. Bob Hopkins, who had neither played nor been a head coach in the NBA, had replaced a basketball legend in Bill Russell. Les remained grateful to Hopkins, "who gave me a great career," but their coaching styles were not compatible. The upbeat, optimistic, positive reinforcement that was the bedrock of Les's philosophy did not mix with a more negative approach taken by Hopkins. Les recalled, "The guys wouldn't play for him. And in the pros, more than in college, if the guys don't play for you, it's over for you as a coach."

By this time, Lenny Wilkens had returned to the Sonics as director of player personnel. He later wrote of the team he had assembled, "As the season began, I didn't think we were a championship-caliber team, but I thought we'd be much better than people expected." He was "eager to sit back and watch all the pieces come together." But that didn't happen. Things soon went from bad to worse. Wilkens observed that Hopkins "was continually ripping his own players" in the press. When they "kept reading in the paper every day that their own coach thought they stunk," they began to believe it and "lost confidence."

Owner Sam Schulman lost confidence faster than the players. When the team's record sank to 5-15, general manager Zollie Volchok implored Wilkens to take the coaching job. He resisted. In their next game, they lost at home to the hapless New Jersey Nets as the fans booed them zealously. In November, when they went on the road to

Kansas City and their record fell to 5-17, Wilkens finally agreed to take over the thoroughly disheartened team.

Les recalled that on the day following the seventeenth loss, he was summoned to Zollie Volchok's hotel room. "I went to the door and Zollie opened it, and there's Lenny. Well, I knew obviously something had happened, and Zollie said, 'Bob Hopkins is gone, and Lenny's going to be the head coach.' Up to that point, I didn't know, *Am I gone too, with Hopkins, or am I going to stay?* Zollie said, 'And Lenny wants you to stay on.'"

Les was absolutely elated by the news, and later said, "Even though everybody said we had a terrible team, we didn't." The season start had been dreadful, but things soon changed. He remembered that from Kansas City they went on to Boston. "And we beat Boston in the Garden. We had the two reporters from the *Times* and the *P-I* with us, and I told them that night, 'We're going to be in the playoffs.' And they just laughed and laughed, and I said, 'I'll bet you whatever you want that we're going to be in the playoffs.'"

The team heard little more booing at home from then on as the city witnessed a truly monumental turnaround by the Sonics. Not only did they go to the playoffs that year, they went all the way to the NBA finals before losing to the Washington Bullets.

When asked what was the key to the 1977-78 season turnaround, Les's reply was simple: "It was Lenny." Wilkens, he said, "brought a different approach to the game. It was much less volatile—less critical, more encouraging. He created an atmosphere of 'we can do this.' He was positive, he wasn't a screamer, and the guys relaxed more."

When Wilkens was asked about his decision to keep Les on as his assistant, he said, "Anytime you're trying to have success at something, you surround yourself with strength. And that's what I see in Les—a lot of strength." For his part, Les said, "What helped me with Lenny is that I knew what I had wanted from an assistant when I was head coach. I never overstepped my role. I knew where to stop—where the head coach takes over, and where I stop."

A COMMON COMMITMENT

Les Habegger and Lenny Wilkens had known each other for a long time. Wilkens had been a popular presence at the basketball camp on Whidbey Island, and when they got together in the NBA, Les said, "We formed a tremendous relationship, and we worked together as a team." The two men approached basketball the same way, and their egos were not on the line. Les felt that their mutual respect permeated the whole Sonics team and was a major factor in the team's success.

Les brought his whole-part-whole coaching approach with him to the Sonics, and he was able to introduce it in practices. "Lenny was a player in the pros, a tremendous player, and he knew the pro game, where, in those days, the idea of breakdown was foreign." But Wilkens knew the value of execution and was open to his assistant's ideas. Les recalled, "If I'd say something, he'd listen. He let me do a lot of things in practice that I used in the college game. The players went along, and we broke things down into their component parts."

During the course of a game, Les kept a notebook, which at the time was something of an innovation on NBA coaching staffs. He said, "So much goes on in the game—and you can't see everything," so he jotted down patterns he saw forming in the action on the court, noted who did or did not take shots, and who had the hot hand. To explain how he transferred this information into the game, he offered a hypothetical example: "I might say, 'Lenny, Jack Sikma hasn't had the ball for the last four or five minutes. We've got to get him the ball.' So he'd run a play for Jack."

Les did not hesitate to give suggestions. He said, "Lenny

wouldn't always take it, but a lot of times he did." He always got a hearing during games and practice sessions. Frank Furtado, the team's trainer and traveling secretary, observed the rapport between the two coaches and later said, "Wilkens did give Habegger a lot of leeway."

Les and Lenny had much in common beyond their commitment to team play and loyalty to their players. Both had been raised in a religious environment—Wilkens as the son of a devout Catholic mother; both had known privation; and basketball had offered both a way out. Coaches Howard Brandberry and Lake Glendenning had given Les great encouragement and a sense of the world outside of Berne, Indiana. Lenny remained loyal to Father Thomas Mannion, the beloved priest who had taken him from the streets of Bedford-Stuyvesant in Brooklyn, put him into basketball, and ultimately secured his scholarship at Providence College.

Both men had served in the army. Wilkens's stint had come in 1961-62, following his graduation from Providence, seventeen years after Les's ordeal in the mountains of Alsace. And their friendship endured for decades beyond their coaching days together.

Frank Furtado recalled that Wilkens emphasized off-court compatibility with the Sonics. "He always liked to have the staff eat dinner together when we were on the road." Compatibility on the road was important, because their location in the upper reaches of the Pacific Northwest meant the Sonics traveled farther than any other team.

Les recalled those grueling years with the Sonics in the days before charter flights and team-owned planes: "We were on the road two weeks at a time and never got home. We'd be back on the East Coast, you know, living in hotels, living out of suitcases, and it became a real grind. We were always flying commercial, so we'd sit in the airport and wait for a flight. The NBA rule was you had to take the first flight out, because you would play the same day. You might be playing in Phoenix tonight, and the next night you're in Houston, and if you didn't get there because you missed a flight, you got fined. So every flight, practically, was a 6:00 a.m. flight to get there in time. We sat in airports by the hour on a trip like that."

In remembering those early-morning departures, exhausting travel, back-to-back games, and home-crowd pressure, he added, "Then again, there was the paycheck."

Free time on the road would often hang heavy. Les devoted his to watching television, shopping, or sightseeing. He laughed as he recalled a memorable trip back east for a game with the Knicks. "In those days, I was a runner. I ran miles every day, and every town we went into I'd get up early and I'd run. I ran all over the United States—literally. We were in New York one time, in November, and I always ran in Central Park. On this particular day, I was out there, and it was cold. I had on a big, heavy coat, and I had a wool cap over my head, and I was running with my head down." It occurred to him that there was no traffic, and he thought that was strange, "But I was running hard, and I wasn't looking, and pretty soon I hear a voice, 'You dumb so-and-so, get off the street!'" He looked up in time to find himself crossing the finish line of the New York Marathon, well up in the pack, "and with everyone screaming and yelling at me."

A Christian Coach in the NBA

Life in the NBA presented greater challenges to Les's conscience, principle, and moral code than anything he had encountered since World War II. "I had entered coaching as a kind of a ministry to help kids—to help guys grow up and become good Christian men. That was my goal, and that was my mission. That's why I went to Seattle Pacific. Going to the Sonics, it was not. The goal was, 'Hey, win games!' and delving into the players' personal lives—that was none of your business. Whether they got in on time at night, what they ate, who they chased around with, who they would see—that was all none of my business. Only to the extent that it affected the way they played."

As for bringing Christian goals to bear in the professional game, he could not say that he affected anyone. Once, when asked about Christianity at the pro sports level, Les replied, "Being a Christian does not result in being a better coach, although it can." He cited the Genesis account of Creation, and went on to say, "I believe it is a lifelong process to discover and understand what it means that I am created in the image of God . . . to realize my full potential and bring that out in others."

Recalling that life in the NBA was a complete change for him, he said, "All through our culture, wherever you are, there are temptations, but there are certainly far more personal temptations in the professional ranks than there were at Seattle Pacific." The Sonics' celebrity and success brought hangers-on, or groupies. Les said, "Everybody clamored after the players." After musing about temptation, he said, "A Christian man is not without sin," but he felt that his faith had kept him from succumbing to a lot of the temptations that beset professional athletes at every turn.

One thing that had dumbfounded the small-town Amish boy from Indiana was his newfound fame. He had never considered himself a celebrity, and said, "I never got over the fact that somebody wanted my autograph. I mean, that's ridiculous! But it happened all the time. You go to a restaurant and you're recognized, and people see you on the street and they stop you. We were in the public eye." This made him conscious of the image he was going to "present to kids." He had been well-known in Seattle as a college coach, but life with the Sonics was "totally different" from how it had been at Seattle Pacific.

After the magical turnaround and near miss of 1978, the next season was greeted with great anticipation in Seattle. "It's a funny thing," Les recalled. "I really am a strong believer in the positive— motivation, self-image, self-esteem, visualization. I practiced those over and over for myself in those days, and I remember that championship year thinking that we were going to win the championship. I really, honestly, believed it, and I was not at all surprised when we did. I just knew that we were going to win it.

"We had a good team, and we started out strong. We started off 10-0, and then we went to Philadelphia, where our starting center at that time, Tom LaGarde, busted his knee. Jack Sikma was playing power forward in those days, and now Jack moved into the center. We revamped our lineup, but we just kept going, and going, and going.

"In the course of a long season, when you see each other every day, there are days when you get up in the morning and you head out to the bus to go to the airport and you say, 'Oh geez, I'm tired of seeing you guys. Get out of my sight.' They don't say it, but everybody feels that way.

"We were in Kansas City on one of those days. We had lost a couple of games, and guys were bickering about nothing in particular—just fussing about different things. And I remember Paul Silas coming to me, and he was fussing—I don't remember what it was—but he was mad enough that it was causing problems on the team. So I went to Lenny that day, and said, 'Lenny, we've got to have a team meeting.' He said, 'Why? What's going on?' And so I told him, 'Paul's upset, and some of the other guys are upset. It's been a long season.' I mean, it was February, or whatever it was. And so he said, 'Okay, call the players.' So we had a squad meeting. Cleared the air. I don't remember exactly what was said, but it was one of those times when things just worked, and it catapulted us into the rest of the season to win games. Those things happen."

WINNING IT ALL

After Lenny and Les coached the Western Conference team to a 134-129 victory over the East in the NBA all-star game in Detroit, the Sonics went on to win the Pacific Division title.

After drawing a first round bye in the divisional playoffs, they dispatched the Los Angeles Lakers four games to one, and moved on to face the Phoenix Suns for the Western Conference championship. Les had that series engraved in his memory.

"We played the first two games in Seattle and beat them easily. We go down there to Phoenix, and they beat us the first game. Then they beat us the second game. So now it's two to two, and we come back up here for game five. They beat us here in Seattle to make it three in row. Now they're ahead three games to two. One more win back at their place, and *they* go to the finals, not us. I'll never forget the flight down to Phoenix that day. Sam Schulman and his wife, Sylvia, were along. I sat with Sylvia, and all the way down she said she was afraid of what's going to happen to Sam if we lose this game. In other words, we'd better win it."

The team did not need any more pressure going into the Sun's arena, where the air vibrated with home team confidence and assurance.

"We get to Phoenix and they already had printed T-shirts that said Western Conference Champions, 1979. I knew the head coach at Phoenix, John MacLeod, and his assistant, Al Bianchi—I knew them well, and so I chatted with them before the game. When I left, they said, 'Well, have a nice summer.'"

When Paul Silas, the battle-tested veteran, heard this, he had something to say to his teammates.

"Paul had already finished dressing, and he was pacing back and forth. Guys were sitting there, and Paul was pacing. Then he stopped, and he looked at the guys, and I won't use the language he used, but he said, 'If any of you guys are thinking of losing, you've got to go by me before you get out of this building.' And that set the tone—it was do or die for us."

It was Mother's Day, and the mother of Suns' mainstay Paul Westphal sang the national anthem before the game. For the overhyped and overconfident crowd, the game was as good as won. Les recalled the final moments: "We were behind almost the whole game, and we kept fighting back, and fighting back. We finally got up by one point, with one second to go, and Phoenix had the ball under their own basket. They threw the ball in—we did a good job of defending—and they threw it to the last guy they wanted to give it to, but the only guy that was open. Of course, he missed, and we win the game by one. Paul Silas was on the bench with me. He and I jumped off the bench, and we landed at midcourt."

Photographers captured the moment—a Seattle sports classic that became known as The Habegger Hop. Lieutenant Governor John Cherberg proclaimed the next day "Habegger Hop Day," after seeing television coverage of Les jumping up and down on the floor after the game. Les could well have considered that hop more as a leap of faith, given his absolute conviction that they were championship bound.

Now standing at three games apiece, the series returned to Seattle for the decisive game. In front of another huge home crowd in the Kingdome, the Sonics thrilled the fans with a 114-110 win, and the stage was set for a return match with the Washington Bullets.

The 1979 Sonics team was virtually the same one that had seen the championship slip away on their home court a year earlier. In that season, before Magic Johnson ushered in the era of dominating superstars, they were truly a team. Each man played his assigned role in the Wilkens scheme of things. The starters were guards Gus Williams and Dennis Johnson, center Jack Sikma, and forwards John Johnson and newcomer Lonnie Shelton. Team captain Fred Brown, a long-range sharpshooter nicknamed "Downtown," and the veteran Paul Silas, a defensive Rock of Gibraltar, came off the bench.

The series opened on the Bullets' court in Landover, Maryland. The home team took that game 99-97, and Seattle loyalists talked for years about dubious officiating in the final two seconds. The Sonics won game two, 92-82, and returned to their home court for game three. Because of a scheduling conflict at the Coliseum, their home court was now in the Kingdome, which was built for football and baseball and had a seemingly limitless seating capacity. In front of 35,000 fans, the Sonics poured in 105 points to Washington's 95, in a game many considered more lopsided than the score indicated. The hard-fought fourth game turned into a true nail-biter, with the Sonics winning 114-112 in overtime. Now leading three games to one, the Sonics made the coast-to-coast flight one more time.

During the 1978 series, after a Washington loss, Bullets coach Dick Motta had uttered an immortal line: "The opera isn't over 'til the fat lady sings." Although an insult to every Wagnerian soprano in the world, the witticism caught on and was resurrected for the 1979 championship round. This year, however, would end in the Bullets' own *Gotterdammerung* when the Sonics secured their fourth straight win in another heart-stopping finish. With fifteen seconds to go, the Bullets, down 95-93, were forced to foul. When Gus Williams calmly sank both free throws to ice the win, 97-93, joyous bedlam erupted on the Seattle bench.

Three decades later, Les clearly recalled his own emotions at the moment the final horn sounded. "I can feel it to this day. Everybody on our team jumped off the bench and were celebrating, but the very first thing that hit me was a Scripture verse: 'He who loses his life will find it, and he who tries to save his life will lose it.'

"I risked literally everything in leaving Seattle Pacific. I went to an unknown situation, to the professional ranks, and I didn't know how I was going to do, or if I'd survive. I risked not only my career, but my life. And so, winning the championship, right or wrong, somehow validated the fact that, 'Hey, you risked, but you won!'"

Ending his tenured academic career and leaving behind faculty friends had been traumatic. Going to the Sonics had been a gamble. But those had been his decisions. Now, in the championship moment, he saw them affirmed as the right choices.

Reflecting further on his years with the Sonics, he said, "In our culture, some people think of you as a celebrity if you're in the professional ranks. So I was asked to do a lot of speaking to a lot of different organizations—at churches, but also regular businesses. And I always emphasized the idea that you risk—you take the leap of faith."

Les enjoyed those Sonics teams immensely. "Winning is music to any coach's ear," he had said earlier in his career, "but the music becomes a real symphony when the game is played and won by men who also live their lives well." Looking back at that championship team, he said, "That's the way it was with the Sonics—we had good men. Good people. And it was a pleasure for me."

FLASHBACK IN FRANCE

Back-to-back championships are always rare, and the following season saw the Sonics fall victim to what Lenny Wilkens called "championship fallout." Some players retired, age took its toll on others, and some said they were just not as hungry as they'd been during the 1979 season. Even so, the Sonics won fifty-six games and took the Los Angeles Lakers to five games before losing the best-of-seven Western Conference playoffs. The coaching duo of Wilkens and Habegger remained the same, but by 1981, contract disputes and further player trades put the Sonics in the basement of the Pacific Division.

Longtime general manager Zollie Volchok retired in late spring of 1983. Les recalled that "Lenny and Zollie and I flew down to meet with Sam in Los Angeles after the season, and that's when Schulman asked me to be his GM." Les became the Sonics' general manager in June of 1983, armed with nineteen years of experience as a college athletic director.

Just before the 1983-84 season, Sam Schulman sold the Sonics to advertising mogul Barry Ackerley. As Les told it, this changed everything. "I was general manager in '83-84 and '84-85. Then Ackerley made a change—he made Lenny quit coaching, and made him general manager, and I became director of player personnel for a year. But Ackerley didn't know anything about the game of basketball, and so I really couldn't function."

The new owner installed his own administrators, but Les stayed on through the 1986 season, which saw further player departures and the destruction of the championship team's core.

The summer of 1984, though, presented a high point in the course of all the changes. As Les recalled, "Lenny and I took the team to Europe. I organized a tour, through a friend of mine who was living in Germany, for the team to play several games over there." Fred Brown and Paul Silas had retired, and the games provided a chance for the coaches to assess several of the new, young players during what amounted to a preseason exhibition schedule.

The Sonics flew to Frankfurt and then moved on to smaller cities, staying in German homes as well as in hotels, and seeing a lot of the country. Players' wives and significant others joined the team and enjoyed such highlights as a Rhine River cruise and a tour of the cathedral in Cologne. Adidas underwrote the trip, providing a Mercedes bus that took the team down through Austria, and into Italy via the Brenner Pass. The team played games as far south as Venice; and on the return trip from Italy up into Switzerland, they stayed a few nights on Lake Geneva. Another highlight was flying into a still-divided Berlin to play a West German team on its side of the wall. After what Les described as "a marvelous time," they flew out of Frankfurt on September 7 and back home to Seattle.

Les, Anne, and Julie had flown to Europe two weeks ahead of the team and had rented a car in Frankfurt to drive to Switzerland, where they visited Leissigen, the birthplace of Les's grandmother Steury. They then drove to France and headed to Alsace—through Strasbourg to Saverne.

It had been forty years since Les had been to Alsace with the 70th Infantry Division. He had never talked of the horrors he had seen, but his memories of the war still remained. Along with the grim details—the sights, sounds, and smells of combat—his memory had never shed the anxiety, dread, and terror that had clutched him during those weeks in the ice and snow of the Vosges Mountains.

Four decades later, Les, with his wife and daughter, stayed overnight in Saverne. He later said, "That was the first encounter with my past—in Saverne." During dinner in their hotel dining room that evening, a plane flew overhead, and Les recalled, "My heart began to race and pound. I got up from the table and went outside, because I thought at the moment I was having a heart attack. I walked all around, and went upstairs to the room to lie down, to hopefully be quiet."

The next day, they drove on from Saverne to Bischweiler, then to Niederbronn, and retraced the route that Les and the 274th Medical Detachment had trudged along through the snow. "We drove down that road, and when we got closer to Philippsbourg I began to see stuff. . . . it was like yesterday. . . because nothing had changed. I recognized everything." The years evaporated, and he was again a frightened nineteen-year-old medic.

As they neared Philippsbourg, he saw the site of their first aid station. "There it was, the place where we had taken in the wounded." Passing that point, they drove by "88 Corner" and on to the house where they had located their second aid station upstairs above the cattle stalls. Again, four decades melted away.

"I saw the aid station—it looked like we'd just left it from combat—and saw the marks from the machine guns and from shrapnel. You could still see it. And I slammed on the brakes of the car. It was the most—this is terrible—but it was the most real . . . I can't tell you how real it was. I was not just looking at it now; I was *there* again as an eighteen-, nineteen-year-old kid, and I began to weep. It was so graphic—so real. It was like there were still guys with blood all over them in the front, and guys that were dead stacked over there—all of that."

Both Anne and Julie, were completely astonished by Les's reaction. They knew the war had affected him, but he'd never talked about it. Julie said they had had World War II books, and had watched all the movies, but it was there in Philippsbourg that she finally "got it" regarding the war. "It wasn't John Wayne; it wasn't *Twelve-O'clock High.* This had been a real war and a horrible experience for my dad."

As they stood there quietly reflecting, a man approached them from a house across the street. Many American veterans had returned to visit Philippsbourg, and he knew immediately that Les was another. He spoke only French, but his wife spoke German and invited them in for coffee. They learned that she had grown up in that house. As Les said, "She had been a little eight- or nine-year-old girl when we were there, and she and her family lived in the basement in 1944." She produced letters from veterans and showed Les a book with names of others who had returned. Les took down some of the names and addresses; this chance meeting would put him back in touch with former Trailblazer comrades.

Les considered the return to Philippsbourg "the most poignant part of the trip, because Philippsbourg was where I should have gotten killed many times." His voice trailed off repeatedly as he later mused, "Whatever the mind does to you—now, to get in my car and drive that route was the most frightening thing I did. It was—and I remember racing out of town with my daughter and my wife."

They traveled on north and west to other areas the 274th had driven through against the Germans—Kreutzberg Ridge, Forbacherberg Ridge, Etzlingen, Spicheren, Spicheren Heights, Stiring-Wendel—and crossed the Saar River. It was August, the weather was nearly perfect, and Les recalled "sitting in Saarbrucken, in a nice little outside café, and thinking, 'Last time I saw this, it was a pile of rubble. Nothing was standing.'"

On their incredible journey through Alsace, the Habeggers had for a brief time confronted decades-old ghosts. But those were soon consigned to the past again. Julie went home, and Les and Anne joined the Sonics in Frankfurt for their fun-filled excursion.

Les was jolted back to reality again when he returned to Seattle for another Sonics season as part of the Ackerley regime. At the end of the 1984-85 season, the Sonics' owner wanted to make some changes. "He wanted a new coach," Les said. "He wanted Lenny to be general manager and made me director of player personnel, and Bernie Bickerstaff became the head coach." Les had known that Ackerley would want to install his own people, and so it came as no surprise when, after that season, his contract wasn't renewed, and Lenny Wilkens left for Cleveland. After a brief period of unemployment, Les was contacted by the Milwaukee Bucks; and in the spring of 1986, he joined coach Don Nelson's staff.

In the two years since the Sonics' splendid European tour, Les had also received overtures from basketball people in Germany. Karl Steiner, owner of the professional team in Bayreuth, had written to him several times. As Les put it, "They were trying to talk me into coming over to coach. I kept turning them down because I wanted to stay in the NBA." He heard from them again while he was the assistant coach in Milwaukee. When Don Nelson told him that he planned to leave the Bucks at the end of the 1986-87 season, Les knew it meant he would be going, too. He remembered wondering, "Do I want to go through this again? . . . If the Germans want to match the money I need, maybe I should go over there for a year." He entered negotiations with Steiner Bayreuth, and when they agreed on a contract, Les went over to Germany, "rather than go fight with some other NBA team."

Once again, as one door closed another opened. Les had seen his departure from Seattle Pacific as a tremendous risk, but it had sent him on to a successful stint in the professional ranks. With his choice to leave the NBA, he again took a risk—one that placed him on the international stage of European basketball.

CHAPTER TWELVE

LIFE AFTER THE NBA:
A RETURN TO GERMANY

B asketball was comparatively slow to gain popularity in Europe. A national league was formed in Germany in 1939, but that first year's national championship was also the last until postwar competition resumed in 1947. Nearly two more decades would pass before West Germany would show emerging strength on the European basketball scene. A professional league, the Basketball Bundesliga, came into being in 1966, and after European television began carrying some NBA games, German teams eagerly sought out coaches with NBA experience.

Les transferred his NBA coaching cachet to the Bundesliga in 1987. Late that spring, he signed on as head coach of Steiner Bayreuth, a team bearing the name of its sponsor, Steiner Optic GmbH, a firm that manufactured high quality binoculars.

Europe's basketball season began in late summer, with training camps and exhibition games beginning in August, and regular league play starting in September. A tour of Southeast Asia had already been scheduled for Steiner Bayreuth by the time Les arrived in mid-June. He learned that the team was to play later in the month in tournaments in Singapore; Kuala Lumpur, Malaysia; and Taipei, Taiwan. Playing against teams from all over the world, they more than held their own. But in the tournament final in Singapore, they lost to the Russians. They flew on to Taipei for what Les called "one of the most prestigious tournaments in the world at that time"—the Jones Cup. Again playing against a wide international field, Steiner Bayreuth reached the finals, where they met an American entry—a Vanderbilt University team that boasted a future NBA star or two. Les still showed traces of pride, decades, later when he said, "We beat them for the championship; we were champions of the Jones Cup, and it was an unbelievable feat."

In 1987, few had ever heard of Germans playing basketball, so the success of the Bayreuth team really was remarkable—and Les's star rose quickly. "With an NBA coach there," he said, "basketball all of a sudden became big, and the reporters and everybody started following me around. I became somewhat of a celebrity . . . and I had a very good team." After they won the Jones Cup in Taipei, he said, "I was king of Germany. I could have been the chancellor."

Les knew well what an assistant coach could contribute. He said, "When I was a head coach in Germany, I didn't have an assistant. I needed somebody to help me, but I didn't have it over there." There was a young German fellow who lived in Bayreuth, who came in and helped some. Les trained him a bit for the assistant's role, but continued to shoulder virtually the entire coaching load himself.

The fact that he spoke German counted for a great deal, especially in postgame question and answer sessions. He said that fans would stay on to listen, "and I did all that in German, of course, rather than in English, and on television and radio—I did everything in German." When he first arrived, he was often taken to be Swiss rather than American, because of his Swiss-German dialect. As he listened closely to people talking in restaurants and on the street, he became alert to words he did not recognize. He jotted them down, sometimes asked how they were spelled, and later found them in his German dictionary. He compiled a personal vocabulary, and thus, as he said, "I taught myself the real German."

Language presented no barrier on the court for the coach, but it did for his American players. As he recounted, "The way it worked in Germany at that time was you were allowed two Americans on your team." American players were also eligible if either parent had been born in Germany. So the Bayreuth team included two Americans and three others whose parents were German-born, giving him five guys who had experience at the collegiate level in the United States. Most of the native German players had learned English at school and they could converse. So when Les talked to the team, he spoke in English. Otherwise, everything was in German. The officials were all German—and Les had quickly learned the German word for referee, "so I could yell at the referees in German."

Winning the Cup and the Cold War

Les relished his years in Bayreuth, saying, "It was a very good experience. The Germans gave me a house, a place to live—and they gave me a car and my salary. The population in Bayreuth was about 75,000, something like that, and I became a celebrity." The late-summer start of the Bundesliga season coincided with the Bayreuth Festival, which drew throngs of opera lovers for sold-out performances of Wagner. Nothing attests to Les's celebrity more than when the mayor of Bayreuth told him, "We have a waiting list of ten years for Festival tickets, but if you want one, I'll get you one." But because the basketball and opera schedules conflicted, Les had to decline the offer.

He did, however, rub shoulders with the opera world, in a sense. He said, "I would hang out at a restaurant that was directly across the street from the opera house—Hollander Stugen was the name of the place; and the owner and I became good friends." One wall of the restaurant was covered with portraits of past and present Wagnerian greats, and in the middle of that wall hung a large picture of Les Habegger. He also met some of the current divas and male singers. "I'd go in there to eat, and all these performers would be in there."

In addition to the German championship, Steiner Bayreuth played for what they called "the cup," or the Pokal. Les described the Pokal as an open tournament that included both club and professional teams. In his first Bayreuth season, 1987-88, Saturn Koln, the Bundesliga entry from Cologne, defeated Steiner Bayreuth for the German title. "But then we turned around and beat them for the cup." The following year, Steiner Bayreuth won both the national championship and the Pokal—the cup. This victory sent them on to play against the other European champions. "We played in Greece, we played in Yugoslavia, in Russia, and in Holland, and Finland— we played all over. For me, it was a very good experience." The team did not go to southern France, however. True to the vow he had made as a young medic during the miserable December of 1944, Les Habegger never returned to Marseille.

In their drive to the 1989 German championship, a five-game series with Leverkausen had proved pivotal, and Les's will to win had propelled Steiner Bayreuth to victory. Down two games to none, they had been thoroughly intimidated in the first half of game three. Les recalled that he really lit into the team at the break. He countered any thoughts the players may have had that they couldn't win three in a row. He emphasized that it was now a one-game series and demanded that they refocus on the job at hand. In the second half, Steiner Bayreuth found its game, came back, and took game three. With their focus and concentration restored, they played each of the next two as "one game series," and went on to capture the title.

German reunification came in 1989, but the Bundesliga had a team in West Berlin while the city was still divided by the infamous wall.

Bayreuth was near the border with East Germany, and Les recalled that to play in Berlin, "We had to drive through East Germany, go through the checkpoints and through customs, where they'd give you a hard time. Then we'd drive into Berlin, play the game, and drive back to Bayreuth," which was about a four-hour drive.

After their championship season, when Steiner Bayreuth played all the national champions, the Russians required the team to fly from an Eastern bloc airport to reach cities that lay behind the Iron Curtain. "So we had to drive to East Berlin to get on a Russian airplane. We flew on Aeroflot out of East Berlin to Russia."

Julie Habegger, who was now a young woman in her mid-twenties, visited her father during that round of games. She traveled with the team to the Soviet-bloc venue in Kaunas, Lithuania, and as the only female in the contingent was listed on the team's roster as its washerwoman. Les was more than a little worried when, at the Aeroflot checkpoint in Berlin, he saw his daughter taken away to be searched. To his great relief, she rejoined the team unharmed. They flew into Minsk, boarded a bus, and traveled overland to their game in Kaunas, "where we played an unbelievable team. Their center, Arvydas Sabonis, played for the Portland Trailblazers for many years. There were several players over there then who later became players in the NBA."

With the Cold War still freezing East-West relations, the United States Army continued to patrol the border from its post just outside Bayreuth. It was there that Les could renew his ties to the English-speaking world and resume his customary pattern of Sunday worship. His status as a veteran allowed him onto the post, where he could get reading material in English. The post chaplain conducted Sunday services, and Les would go to chapel. "Once in a while I went to a German church, which would be Evangelical, but most of the time I went out there to the chapel."

Les recalled watching television in his Bayreuth apartment the day the wall dividing Germany came down in 1989."They showed demonstrations occurring in Leipzig and Dresden. I'm watching this and thinking, *Wow, what's this?* They showed clips of Gorbachev and the East German leader, Honegger—those two guys together. And I'm thinking, *Whoa,* and watching all this on TV. And then, in a day or so, Honegger resigned. I saw the whole thing unfold. . . . People from the East were coming across in droves."

Bayreuth, near the former border, was one of the first towns to receive the human tidal wave. The government of West Germany had promised a cash allowance (something in the neighborhood of ten marks) to those who crossed over. Les recalled that his landlord, who worked in a bank, said, "We've got blocks long of people lined up in our bank, waiting to get the ten marks and buy something." Les watched the arrival of the now officially free East Germans, including hordes on an unprecedented buying spree that stripped the merchandise from Bayreuth's stores. One scene outside the fruit and vegetable market where he shopped stayed with him.

"Several women were outside there looking in the windows, and I said to the owner, 'What's this?' He said, 'Those are East Germans. They have never seen a banana—have no idea what that is.' And they were looking at bananas and other stuff."

On the team's next trip to Berlin, Les went to the wall and found that they'd knocked holes in it, and people were going back and forth through the wall. He retrieved a piece of the old barrier for himself as a memento of the Cold War.

Les's experience in the hot war that had come before the Cold War resurfaced again in Bayreuth. His next-door neighbor there had been drafted into the German Army in 1938, and he frequently recounted tales of World War II. Les had not shared that he had been in the U.S. Army until his new German friend mentioned towns in Alsace and said he had been in Bischweiler on December 31, 1944. Amazed at the coincidence, Les revealed that he, too, had been in

Bischweiler that New Year's Eve. They could hardly believe it. They commiserated a bit and agreed that no one would ever know what they had experienced.

TRANSITIONS AND CONCLUSIONS

In his three years as Steiner Bayreuth's head coach, Les had been regarded as "the American basketball legend Les Habegger," as the *Berliner Zeitung* called him. But he began to think, *I just don't want to be here alone.* Julie had visited once, and Anne had spent part of a season in Bayreuth, but then she had returned to teaching in Seattle. Les told Steiner Bayreuth, "I don't want to coach anymore." They countered with a plan for him to become general manager and not have to stay in Germany the whole time. He recalled their saying, "Come in the summer when training camp starts, and help us get started with training camp and the exhibition games, and then you can go back to Seattle. And then come again in the late winter before the playoffs start, and stay here for the playoffs." That sounded workable to him, so he accepted their terms and began commuting on an international scale—Seattle to Copenhagen on SAS; on to Frankfurt or Munich; and then back again, several times each season. After five years of this schedule, there came a time when he said to himself, "I don't want to keep on doing this." During his last year with Steiner Bayreuth, they asked him to coach again. He told them, "You don't have enough money to get me to do that." Their reply was: "Try us." Les gave them a figure upwards of $200,000 that he thought there was no way they would meet, but they responded by saying, "Okay."

The team agreed to his salary demand for the 1995-96 season, plus they provided a house and a car and paid his expenses. But things had changed at Steiner Bayreuth. Karl Steiner himself had hired Les in 1987 to coach his team. Now, Les was dealing with a new business manager who, he later said, had promised money the company hadn't budgeted for the team. So, eventually, I wasn't getting paid." Apparently, Les had been right when he told them that they didn't have enough money to get him to coach again. His decision to return to Seattle came easily after that.

But when Les arrived back in the Pacific Northwest, he discovered that, in the words of novelist Thomas Wolfe, you can't go home again. Things had changed in Seattle. The demands of professional basketball had placed intolerable strains on Les's relationship with Anne. The pace of life and the challenge of the international game had been exhilarating for him, while she had maintained a more settled lifestyle at home and had found great satisfaction in her teaching career. When Les returned from Bayreuth in 1995, their marriage ended in divorce.

Scott and Julie had moved on with their own lives. Though Julie still lived in Seattle, Scott had moved to Spokane where he operated a successful veterinary practice. Later, with the family splintered, Les thought that perhaps his decision to leave Germany was ill-advised. "Maybe I should have stayed, and who knows? I'd have been commissioner of who knows what by then."

His NBA credentials, enhanced by his championship ring, had made him a true celebrity in Europe. Back in Seattle, and again unemployed, he slowly realized that unemployed now meant retired. He had recently visited an old friend from Wheaton, a teammate who was living in Arizona. He decided to move there, and ultimately bought a home in the Trilogy Golf Course community near Phoenix.

CHAPTER THIRTEEN

RETIREMENT AND REFLECTION

Most, if not all, retirees know a feeling of emptiness when the longtime focus of their lives is removed. Their jobs had defined who they are. No job is more defining than that of a coach; none offers greater challenge nor presents greater risk. No job allows greater satisfaction than being intensely involved with a sport you love and interacting with athletes of talent and promise. Les had enjoyed a reprieve in Europe. He said, "My years in Bayreuth were a revival in my life. I was back to coaching, and that is what energized me." He now faced the finality of no longer being a coach, and found it very hard to be retired with nothing to do.

He had played golf off and on since his college years, but said his game had never been very good. Now, living in Arizona with access to a course and unlimited time to play regularly, he brought it back to a respectable level. But, ever the perfectionist, he insists, "I don't play as well as I'd like." He bought a bicycle, made good use of the community fitness facilities to work out, and began lifting weights. He remained in excellent physical condition.

After forty years of suppressing the memories of combat, he had experienced an emotional return to World War II sites on the trip through Alsace in 1984. Now, in retirement, he reestablished contact with his fellow Trailblazers. Les found that he was not the only veteran of the 274th Regiment Medical Detachment living in the Phoenix area. It was a true pleasure for him to be reunited with Captain Frank Ellis, the battalion surgeon he so greatly admired.

Les became a regular at 70th Division reunions. At one of the biennial division gatherings, he was able to confirm that he and his neighbor in Bayreuth had been accurate in remembering their whereabouts some four decades earlier. When the 274th had been in Bischweiler on December 31, 1944, German troops had indeed occupied the other end of town.

Veterans of the 70th Division were scattered nationwide, and every year those living in the West came together for what they called "mini reunions." Les and Captain Ellis hosted one such gathering in Scottsdale in 2006, and it had SPC overtones as well for Les. He had been invited to a Seattle Pacific fundraiser that spring, and there he met the army's chief of chaplains, Major General G. T. Gunhus. Chaplain Gunhus is a Seattle Pacific alumnus, class of 1962. Although Les had not known him on campus, the chaplain assured the coach that he certainly knew him and had gone to SPU home games. Les asked General Gunhus if he would consider speaking at the Trailblazers' upcoming reunion. He happily agreed, and his appearance was something of real coup for Frank and Les.

For decades, Les had carried the silent burden of war experiences that defied description. By associating once again with men who had endured those same horrors and had survived, Les found some ease in his memories of World War II.

On his return to Berne, Indiana, in 1946, those memories had been so raw that he could not possibly have shared them with his family. He had seen and done things beyond their comprehension.

Decades later, he still believed that he couldn't have made them understand.

"I left as an eighteen-year-old kid, and the war really took the youth away from us kids. We never had a chance to be adolescents, because the army expected us to grow up and be men right away. So I came home and realized that the experiences in combat had changed me. Now I was a man . . . a different guy than my parents or family knew when I left."

In the pattern of many snowbirds who migrate to Phoenix in the winter, Les now traveled with the seasons. Each summer he returned to the Northwest to visit friends, former colleagues, and family. He happily slipped into the role of a proud grandfather who doted on his three granddaughters. Before returning to the desert one autumn, he considered whether his plans should include going by way of Indiana.

BACK TO HIS ROOTS

The strong Amish pull of family had always been with him. It made his life something of an intellectual and emotional tug-of-war. His father had not understood why he left the family to attend Butler University. Les recalled the same reaction from his father when he and Anne moved out to Seattle Pacific. "He said, 'I don't understand. Why are you doing this? Why are you going so far from home?'" Looking back, Les thought he had missed a great deal by leaving. "Very soon I was gone, and my nephews—my brothers' and sisters' kids—were growing up. And I was gone."

Les and his family had made a number of trips to Berne over the years, and Rosina Habegger had often visited in their Seattle home. She had seen that the Amish heritage was passed to his children by way of her gifts of books and toys and her traditional dishes that Les had always relished. Julie remembered her grandmother as quite the baker. "She made really good date cookies and divinity fudge." Julie herself continues to make her grandmother's Swiss pancakes for her own daughter as a breakfast treat.

Les always had the sense that he had broken away from the family. "Throughout everything I accomplished, the whole time, my feeling was, 'I'm not with the family, and I'm the one who left them.'" He said this had become ingrained. "I was left feeling— longing? homesickness? whatever you want to call it—for the town of Berne, Indiana, and my family. All my brothers and sisters lived in the town—we were all right there together. And so there has always been—I don't know how else to say it, but an ache.

"Looking back, one important thing about my childhood that impacted me greatly all through my professional career—in my coaching career, and in my personal life—was the teaching from my grandfather. I grew up with a profound sense of 'I'm not worth very much.'"

He could never quite believe that the family ever saw him as worthy or capable of accomplishing anything. But they had taken great pride in his accomplishments, had followed his career, and cheered his triumphs.

He came to appreciate what his family had done, however, and expressed true admiration for his parents. He thought perhaps he had been too hard on them in recalling their stern restrictions on him and his siblings. He was nearly in awe that, given their own limited, sixth-grade education, they had enabled those who followed to achieve academically.

Once free of their grandfather's prohibitions, Les, Jesse, and Cliff had graduated from high school. Martha received her diploma as a mature student three decades later, and Joel earned a bachelor's degree. But it is in the next generation that Les finds their greatest legacy. Rosina and Jacob's grandchildren personify excellence. Eighteen of the twenty-one are college graduates, with careers in business, teaching, engineering, medicine, accounting, veterinary medicine, and the ministry. Those holding doctorates include one Nobel laureate. When Martha's son, Richard Schrock, received the prize for chemistry in 2005, his proud mother, then in her ninth decade, journeyed to Stockholm for the award events.

FINDING FAITH AND TAKING RISKS

Fear had been Les's constant companion as a child and as a young adult—fear of his grandfather, fear of damnation, fear of defying custom and tradition, and the fear only those who endure the hell of combat can know. Finding faith and taking risks had been his salvation. Faith had overcome the fear of damnation and an angry God and set him on a course of Christian commitment.

Taking risks had marked his path to success in the world. It had been an enormous risk to defy his father and answer the draft call in 1943. No less a risk took him from Berne to Butler University in the spring of 1949. He risked even more in leaving Butler for an obscure Bible college in Minneapolis for fall semester 1950. After a rewarding four years at Wheaton College, followed by marriage and graduate school at the University of Minnesota, he made perhaps the greatest risk to date—leaving his family in Indiana and moving to the Pacific Northwest. Accepting an offer to teach and coach at Seattle Pacific College, which was virtually unknown to him at the time, constituted no small risk. Neither did the move he made twenty years later, when he "left the protective environment of a Christian college and joined the professional basketball ranks." A national championship in that realm enhanced his already impressive coaching reputation, and he returned to Europe to risk all that in the fledging German basketball league.

His faith sustained him through the risks along his incredible journey. He later mused on the matter of his risk taking. Speaking in the third person, he said, "Answering the question as to why the boy took these risks is not as important as the fact that he did what he did and came through these risks because of his faith."

From the boyhood hours of shooting baskets indoors at home, with the rag ball sewn for him by his mother, and the endless days of aiming at the makeshift hoop in the barn, basketball was a part of Les Habegger's life. It had been his focus for more than sixty years. He had been in the public eye for forty of those years. He had found success at every level, both as player and a coach, and was involved in winning national championships on two continents. When asked what had been the high point of his accomplishments, with the assumption that he would say "the 1979 NBA championship," he smiled, nodded, and replied, "but I wasn't the head coach." As the head coach in Bayreuth he had again been free to mold the team, to drive them to do it his way.

He had gained financially by coaching professional teams, "but I relished the 'chess game' of coaching at the college level and found it more personally rewarding." Long after retiring he said, "I miss Seattle Pacific when I think of coaching." There, he had been able to work toward his primary goal of assisting young Christian men to reach their full potential. He had enjoyed what he described as "trying to make a silk purse out of a sow's ear" with the SPC program.

What he considers his greatest basketball thrill did not come on the court; it came in January 2004 when he was inducted into Seattle Pacific's Athletic Hall of Fame. As the program for the induction dinner proclaimed, "Winning basketball is the legacy of Les Habegger's nineteen years at Seattle Pacific." He was overwhelmed, but delighted, that sixty of his former players were on hand to honor him. This affirmed for him "that I had accomplished something" — a rare moment of self-satisfaction for a man who still had lingering doubts about his own worth.

AFTERWORD

I was thrilled to hear that a book was being written about my college coach, Les Habegger.

I had the privilege of playing for Les and have kept in regular contact with him over the past thirty-four years. Coach had more energy, drive, and enthusiasm than most of his players, even though many of us stood almost a foot taller.

Memories from my college days are marked by Coach's intensity, preparation, and creativity. He was not unlike other Hoosier-bred coaches who have paced the hardwood. He will be remembered for his commitment to practice, visualization, and repetition. He was also quick to adopt successful strategies, such as the run and jump defense or the four corner offense made famous by Phil Ford when he played for Dean Smith at North Carolina. Coach Smith spoke at one of Les's basketball camps at Camp Casey. I met Coach Smith on an airplane in the mid-1970s and he spoke very highly of Les Habegger's disciplined approach to the game.

Due to Coach's relationship with Bob Houbregs through their basketball camps, Seattle Pacific hosted the Seattle Sonics' summer training. In addition, most visiting NBA teams coming to Seattle to play the Sonics would work out in Royal Brougham Pavilion (our home court, named in honor of a noted Seattle sportswriter).

I can remember watching the visiting teams work out. Kareem Abdul-Jabbar (then of the Milwaukie Bucks, prior to moving to L.A. to play for the Lakers); Bob Lanier and Dave Bing of the Detroit

Pistons; Julius Irving; Connie Hawkins, and the list goes on. This was all a result of Les's influence in the community. After one of our grueling practices, it was fun to watch these pros go through their shootarounds on the same court where we practiced and conditioned.

When Lenny Wilkens was traded to Cleveland (a very unpopular move to the Seattle fan base), he worked out in our gym to stay in shape while the two teams worked out the details of his contract and the trade.

Les's teams from the earliest days were distinguished by their hard work, physical and mental conditioning, execution of fundamentals, defense, rebounding, and repetition. His 1965 team was perhaps his finest group of players. Names like Howard Heppner, Dave and Gary Wortman, Terry Fein, John Crow, Dave Rumppe, and Gary Habegger were engrained in our memories of Coach's best years.

Along with my teammates, I was fortunate enough to play in Les's final season at the helm of the Fighting Falcons, who fought it out in the gym on Nickerson, "the little school by the canal."

As an NCAA Division II independent at the time, we had no conference championship game, which would have sent the victor to a postseason appearance and a chance to go to the Big Dance in Evansville, Indiana. The University of Evansville Purple Aces, under their Hall of Fame coach, Arad McCutcheon, were a perennial Division II basketball powerhouse. Coach got us the opportunity to play a home-and-home series with them, which we split. Don Buse, a future NBA player for the Indiana Pacers, played for Evansville at that time.

Coach Habegger had big wins against many Northwest powers, including Seattle University during their heyday; University of Portland; Portland State; Gonzaga; Puget Sound; the Washington state schools, including Central, Western, and Eastern, as well as other nationally ranked teams such as UC Riverside, Irvine, Sacramento State, St. Mary's, and the Purple Aces of Evansville. Coach's teams were always competitive.

It was a privilege to play for Les alongside guys known as Bals, Borts, Hads, Hills, Weeds, Peels, Stoney, and Jonesie. If your name could be pluralized, it was; if not, you got a nickname. We dared not refer to Les as Habs (although it fit the plural rule). Coach, or Coach Habegger, was the appropriate greeting. For us baby boomers whose fathers had served in the military, we obliged the formality.

In 1974, Coach left the comfort of SPU for a well-earned year of sabbatical, which he used to learn from other great coaches in the field, and to reflect on the future. Little did he know that 1974 would be his last season as head coach of the Falcons.

Those of us who understood him, and appreciated his intensity and approach to the game, always knew that Coach had something to offer at the next level—whether at a Division I school or in the professional ranks. His storybook rise from a humble start, as the youngest of ten children from a little town in northern Indiana, to the pinnacle of the professional game as part of the 1979 NBA champions, made us all proud to say we had played for him.

As players, we didn't know much about his earlier years and experiences. Although he did talk about foxholes a lot, none of us players had ever been in one.

Many times over the last thirty years, I have had a chance to stay in touch with Coach. I remember watching the Sonics in Indianapolis shortly after the Pacers joined the NBA from the rival ABA. Coach and I had dinner prior to a game in Oakland when the Sonics were in town to play the Warriors. Prior to the game, he introduced me to Jack Sikma (whom I had played against when he was an underclassmen at Illinois Wesleyan), Wally Walker, Fred Brown, Paul Silas, and Lenny Wilkens.

Coach demonstrated the character he tried to pass on to us. He took an adverse situation (the premature ending of his career at Seattle Pacific), and turned it into a second career with the Seattle Supersonics. It was fun to watch the Sonics run variations of the same offense we'd run at SPU. I remember the first time I saw them run a variation of Diagonal. In their version of the play Fred Brown would dish the ball off to Johnnie Johnson and then come around a double screen on the baseline set by Jack Sikma and Lonnie Shelton, only to get the ball back for a jumper from the corner. In my days at SPU, Carey Weedman (and others before him) executed that same play time and again in our games. When Jack Sikma came off a screen in Guard Through, I imagined Jim Ballard coming off a Bob Jones screen a hundred times and gently lofting the ball through the hoop with ease. It all went to show that Coach had something to offer at the next level. He and Lenny Wilkens ran variations of the plays that suited their players' individual skills.

With many of Les's former players, what started out as a teacher/ student or coach/player relationship became one of a well-respected mutual friendship. Some of the best times I remember with Coach have been on the golf course, enjoying a good cigar, having dinner with a nice bottle of wine, or talking endlessly on the phone.

The culmination for many of us was Coach's induction into the Seattle Pacific Sports Hall of Fame. More than sixty of his former players (and friends) attended a dinner to honor and roast our coach and friend the night after his induction ceremony. Some of his players from the late 1950s attended the event. Those of us who were able to attend this grand celebration were there to honor the man we simply called Coach. To us, it was a title of affection and respect.

Les's players went on to careers in a variety of venues. Though many are now retired, a high percentage of Les's players left SPU to become successful teachers, coaches, doctors, dentists, pilots, entrepreneurs, business owners, and the list goes on. The principles of planning, preparation, and execution that Coach taught us on the basketball court are the same principles we apply in our lives and businesses to this day.

We were fortunate to have played for one of the finest coaches in all of modern basketball. We have laughed with him, celebrated successes, and endured defeats. He taught us far more than what we learned on the basketball court.

Les, we love you. Be kind to yourself. You had the opportunity to do what few others have accomplished. You were part of a team that helped to build an NBA championship team.

More importantly, you are a big part of all of our lives. The discipline and focus you built into our lives have contributed to making us into the men we have become—men made in God's image, as you always taught us.

I know I speak for my SPU teammates and many others when I say that we love Les Habegger and are proud to still call him Coach.

—Don DeHart
SPU 1970-74

A Note on Published Sources

Readers interested in more information about topics that provided context and background for this memoir will find much to reward them in the following volumes. It is by no means a complete list of works on the various subjects.

Amish and Mennonite sources include: Donald B. Kraybill, *The Riddle of Amish Culture* (Johns Hopkins University Press, 2001); Donald B. Kraybill and Carl F. Bowman, *On the Backroad to Heaven: Old Order Hutterites, Mennonites, Amish, and Brethren* (Johns Hopkins University Press, 2001); John A. Hostetler, *Amish Society*, 4th ed. (Johns Hopkins University Press, 1993); John A. Hostetler, ed., *Amish Roots* (Johns Hopkins University Press, 1989); James A. Warner and Donald M. Denlinger, *The Gentle People: A Portrait of the Amish* (Mill Bridge Museum, 1969); John A. Hostetler and Gertrude Enders Huntington, *Amish Children: Education in the Family, School, and Community*, 2nd ed. (Harcourt Brace Jovanovich, 1992); Donald B. Kraybill, ed., *The Amish and the State* (Johns Hopkins University Press, 1993); and Steven M. Nolt, *A History of the Amish*. rev. ed. (Good Books, 2003).

Of particular interest for information about the Amish in Indiana are Thomas J. Meyers and Steven M. Nolt, *An Amish Patchwork: Indiana's old Orders in the Modern World* (Indiana University Press, 2005); and John Christian Wenger, "The Mennonites in Indiana and Michigan" in *Studies in Anabaptist and Mennonite History*, no. 10 (Herald Press, 1961). The single most important source for the

Habegger family's church in Berne, Indiana, is Frederick J. Schrock, *The Amish Christian Church: Its History and Legacy* (Ambassador Publishers, 2002).

For general coverage of religion in the twentieth century, see the relevant chapter in Martin E. Marty, *Pilgrims in Their Own Land: 500 Years of Religion in America* (Little, Brown and Company, 1984). Frances FitzGerald, *Cities on a Hill: A Journey through Contemporary American Cultures* (Simon and Schuster, 1991) provides another good overview. More focused on postwar America are Joel Carpenter, *Revive Us Again: The Reawakening of American Fundamentalism* (Oxford University Press, 1997); George M. Marsden, *Understanding Fundamentalism and Evangelicalism* (Eerdmans, 1991); and William G. McLoughlin, Jr., *Modern Revivalism: Charles Grandison Finney to Billy Graham* (Ronald Press, 1959).

The Wheaton College story can be found in Paul M. Bechtel, *Wheaton College: A Heritage Remembered, 1860-1984* (Harold Shaw Publishers, 1984); Edward A. Coray, *Through Clouds and Sunshine: A Story of Wheaton College Athletics from the Beginning: 1892–1939-40* (Wheaton Alumni Association, 1979); and Edward A. Coray, *The Wheaton I Remember* (Books for Living, 1974). The Habegger years at Seattle Pacific are included in Donald McNichols, *A Growing Vision: Seattle Pacific University, 1891-1991*(Seattle, 1991).

A general work on Christian higher education is William C. Ringenberg, *The Christian College: A History of Protestant Higher Education in America* (Eerdmans, 1984). The historical tie between Christianity and sports receives good treatment in Clifford Putney, *Muscular Christianity: Manhood and Sports in Protestant America, 1880-1920* (Harvard University Press, 2001).

The combat in Alsace during the Battle of the Bulge has received little or no attention from historians. The best book available was written by the 274th Infantry's commander, Col. Wallace R. Cheves: *Snow Ridges and Pillboxes: A True History of the 274th Infantry Regiment of the 70th Division in World War II.* Another book covers the entire 70th Division: Edmund C. Arnold, *The Trailblazers: The Story of the 70th Infantry Division* (Seventieth Infantry Division Association, 1989). Among government documents is a short piece: *Ardennes-Alsace: The U.S. Army Campaigns of World War II* (ca. 1994). Further reading on the role of medics can be found in Brendan Phibbs, *The Other Side of Time: A Combat Surgeon in World War II* (Little, Brown and Company, 1987); Patricia W. Sewell, ed., *Healers in World War II: Oral Histories of Medical Corps Personnel* (McFarland & Company, 2001); Albert E. Cowdrey, *Fighting for Life: American Military Medicine in World War II* (Free Press, 1994); and Paul Fussell's excellent *The Boys' Crusade: the American Infantry in Northwestern Europe, 1944-45* (Modern Library, 2003). On the return from war to civilian life, see Michael D. Gambone, *The Greatest Generation Comes Home: the Veteran in American Society* (Texas A&M University Press, 2005). Two works offering panoramic coverage of the entire war are Geoffrey C. Ward and Ken Burns, *The War: An Intimate History, 1941-1945* (Knopf, 2007) and Hal Buell, ed., *The World War II Album: the Complete Chronicle of the World's Greatest Conflict* (Tess Press, 2002).

Books published about basketball and other sports, both college and professional, would fill a sizable wing of a large library. The following are a few that proved useful.

Background for the college scene came from Alexander M. Weyand, *The Cavalcade of Basketball* (Macmillan, 1960); Jack Falla, *NCAA: The Voice of College Sports* (National Collegiate Athletic Association, 1981); Murray Sperber, *Onward to Victory: The Crises That Shaped College Sports* (Henry Holt and Company, 1998); Andrew Zimbalist, *Unpaid Professionals: Commercialism and Conflict in Big-Time College Sports* (Princeton University Press, 1999); and John Wooden with Steve Jamison, *My Personal Best: Life Lessons from an All-American Journey* (McGraw-Hill, 2004).

The Seattle Supersonics coverage includes Blaine Johnson, *What's Happenin'?: A Revealing Journey Through the World of Professional Basketball* (Prentice-Hall, 1978); *World Champions, 1978-1979: Seattle Supersonics* (Moore Publications, 1979); and Michael E. Goodman, *Seattle Supersonics* (Creative Education, 1993). One of the best books on professional basketball is Lenny Wilkens with Terry Pluto, *Unguarded: My Forty Years Surviving in the NBA* (Simon and Shuster, 2000). The story of professional basketball in Germany can best be found by searching the internet for German basketball and Bundesliga.